The One-Minute Philosopher™

Montague Brown, Ph.D.

The One-Minute Philosopher™

Quick Answers to Help You
Banish Confusion, Resolve Controversies,
and Explain Yourself Better to Others

SOPHIA INSTITUTE PRESS®
Manchester, New Hampshire

Copyright © 2001 Montague Brown

Printed in the United States of America

Jacket design by Lorraine Bilodeau

On the jacket: "Man at Chalkboard," Philip Scheuer, illustrator, Copyright © The Stock Illustration Source, Inc.

Sophia Institute Press®
Box 5284, Manchester, NH 03108
1-800-888-9344
www.sophiainstitute.com

Library of Congress Cataloging-in-Publication Data
Brown, Montague, 1952-
    The one-minute philosopher : quick answers to help you banish
      confusion, resolve controversies, and explain yourself better
      to others / by Montague Brown.
    p. cm.
  Includes bibliographical references.
  ISBN 1-928832-25-3 (alk. paper) — 1-928832-55-5 (pbk. : alk. paper)
  1. Philosophy. I. Title.

B72.B695 2001
100 — dc21   00-068762

To my children,
from whom I learn so much

Contents

Introduction

Life can be confusing. Every day brings challenges. Teenagers wonder how they can know whether they're in love. As parents, we try to teach them self-control, but not repression — yet how can we know the difference?

At work or at school, we want to cooperate: this means being obedient but not servile, polite but not phony — but it's hard to know where to draw the line. And we ask ourselves what makes a real leader, instead of a mere popular trendsetter, and where tolerance ends and adherence to standards begins.

The difference between knowing such things and not knowing them can make the difference between happiness and misery. But these days, who has time for studies of such basic things?

That's why I wrote *The One-Minute Philosopher.*

It's for people like you who have too much to do and too little time to do it. It will help you realize how much you already know about reality and your place in it and, at the same time, will help you think more deeply about things, even if you can find only five minutes here and there to do it.

I have purposely not organized this book according to general categories. It is meant to be an invitation to explore. So open it anywhere. On each left-hand page you'll find one concept, and on the right you'll find another that's often confused with it.

As you read, you'll see how things that seem quite similar can turn out to be fundamentally different. Wise men and women see the difference and live happier lives because of what they see.

Because all truths are related, your starting point will ultimately lead you to all the other topics. I've marked with an asterisk those words that have their own treatment elsewhere in the book, and I've included as an appendix a list of other things you can read to learn more about the issues discussed here.

It's true that every one of the words I discuss has other meanings besides the one on which I focus. That's the way language works. So please bear with me if occasionally my understanding of the meaning of a word is not quite the understanding you are used to. My concern here is not so much the meaning of words as the realities represented by words. Sometimes those realities are seen best by considering less familiar meanings of words.

Sure, there's a great deal more that could be said about these topics, but we have to start somewhere: this book is a point of departure. Let it be for you a beginning.

Montague Brown
April 2001

The One-Minute Philosopher™

Admiration

Appreciation of another's good

Admiration recognizes objective *good and rejoices in this recognition. To admire another's good is to be happy that such a good exists and happy that another person has it.

If I am filled with admiration, I see someone else's talent, success, or *virtue as good for both of us. I approve of the person's having the good, and I can see the value of pursuing such a good myself. There is no sense of competition in admiration. The more good another has, the more I can admire. Another person's good makes the world better, and the existence of this good opens my mind to the possibilities for real *excellence. Admiration can inspire me to try to attain the good myself.

We can admire all sorts of goods that another person has. We can admire the person's fancy car or her fine musical instrument. We can admire the person's style of dressing or her taste in furniture. We can admire the person's talent, whether intellectual, athletic, or artistic. And, perhaps most important, we can admire the person's *character, her generosity, her *honesty, her ability to say and do the right thing in all situations. In every case we wish that we had the good thing in question, but we are glad that, if we do not have it, at least someone else does.

Although admiration and envy both recognize rejoices that another has them,

ASK YOURSELF:
Do I appreciate some good thing that another has and wish I had it? Am I happy that the other has it? If so, I am full of admiration.

"Admiration — the power of discerning and taking delight in what is beautiful in visible form and lovely in human character."

John Ruskin
An Idealist's Arraignment of the Age

Envy

Resentment of another's good

Envy recognizes objective *good but is pained by this recognition. To envy another's good is to want that good for ourselves and resent the fact that someone else has it.

If I am envious, I see someone else's talent, success, or *virtue as somehow diminishing me. One of the strange characteristics of envy is that it wishes that the other person did not have the good in question. If I am envious, I see myself in competition with others. There are two ways my position may improve: either I can strive to attain the good myself, or the other person can lose it. Having someone else fail is easier than hard work. In either case, I gain ground.

Any good or apparent good possessed by another may be cause for envy. That another person has material possessions that we lack may cause us to be envious. We can envy someone's talent or success. Why is he such a great musician when I am not? Why was he chosen for the team and not I? We can envy the close *friendship that our friend has with another. Worst of all, we can envy another's good *character. In every case, we wish that we had the good thing in question, but we also wish that, if we can't have it, the other person couldn't have it either.

---

and admire good things, only admiration
whereas envy resents the fact.

⤳

"Men are so jealous of good which they have not themselves accomplished, that a man often makes himself enemies by the simple fact that he has rendered great service."

Toussaint L'Ouverture
In C. L. R. James, The Black Jacobins

ASK YOURSELF:
Do I appreciate some good thing that another has and wish I had it? Am I resentful and wish the other did not have it? If so, I am full of envy.

Authority

The right to rule

An authority is a legitimate source of *power, *knowledge, or *morality. Authoritative power is rightfully endowed by *law or *custom; authoritative knowledge is expertise; moral authority is a matter of *virtue. The good parent exemplifies all these kinds of authority: she has the *right, the *wisdom, and the virtue to rule, and she rules for the *good of her children.

If I refuse to heed someone with more authority than I have, I lose out on an opportunity for growth — whether that growth be moral (as with a parent) or intellectual (as with a teacher) or aesthetic (as with an artistic master). Since most of my knowledge comes from sources other than myself, I would be cutting myself off from intellectual and moral nourishment if I were to ignore authorities. The *choice is mine.

Authorities are all around us. The coach is an authority. When he says, "Do this," we should do it; it will make us better players. Teachers have legal authority to teach and usually have expertise, too. Legally, parents are authorities over children and are, in most cases, worthy of *obedience. In general, their experience and concern for our well-being make it reasonable for us to obey them even when we may not completely understand their directives.

Authority is the right to impose order those who obey; power is

ASK YOURSELF:
Does this person have the right to command? Is this right based on something I can understand and should accept? If so, the person has authority.

"Tyranny is the opposite of authority. For authority simply means right; and nothing is authoritative except what somebody has a right to do, and therefore is right in doing."

G. K. Chesterton
As I Was Saying (1936)

Power

The ability to rule

While authority commands *respect, power commands, period. The reasons and methods for such command are arbitrary. Instead of the respect and trust due an authority, *fear and weakness are the motives for heeding power. The paradigm case of the exercise of power is the *tyrant, who has no *right to rule and rules for his own *good.

If I do not heed someone more powerful than I am, I lose an opportunity, although the opportunity is not for moral, intellectual, or artistic growth but for survival, or perhaps for success in continuing my lifestyle and increasing my comforts and influence. If I obey the power, perhaps the power will empower me. If I disobey, I will suffer the consequences and may ultimately be forced to obey. I have little *choice in the matter.

Some people rule merely by power; others have legal but not *moral authority. An armed man wields power, not authority: we must do what he says, or else. Peer pressure is power, not authority: those who are popular are not therefore right. The teacher who imposes unfair rules has the legal authority to do so, but loses moral authority by being unjust. In these cases, people rely more on power than on intelligence and moral example to get their way.

according to reason and for the good of the ability to enforce our will.

"Men are not corrupted by the exercise of power or debased by the habit of obedience, but by the exercise of a power which they believe to be illegitimate, and by obedience to a rule which they consider to be usurped and oppressive."

Alexis de Tocqueville
Democracy in America, Introduction

ASK YOURSELF:
Does this person command because he can? Does he lack the legal and moral right to command? If so, the person has power but not authority.

Certainty

Intellectual conviction based on evidence

Certainty pertains to *knowledge: it is knowing without doubt that something is so. Certainty is a result of having considered the matter thoroughly and having found sufficient *evidence to justify our position.

Although certainty is something that I have within me, it is outward looking. That is, I appeal to objective criteria to substantiate my position. If I refuse to change my mind, it is because no objective evidence has been given, nor can I conceive of any, that would shake my certainty. Certainty is not a consequence of being proud or overbearing; rather, it is the result of being humble before the truth.

We are certain of many things. Once we understand them, mathematical and logical propositions are certain: 2+2=4; if a=b and b=c, then a=c. We are certain about these because the evidence for them is obvious. Many scientific propositions are equally certain. We are certain that a human being is not a tree and that lead is heavier than water. We also have certainty about some ethical points. We are certain that helping others is better than hurting them, that love is better than hate. In all these examples, certainty is not a matter of being inflexible, but of being convinced by evidence.

Certainty is an intellectual state evidence; inflexibility is a

ASK YOURSELF:
Is my main concern to know the truth? Is my refusal to change my mind based on convincing evidence? If so, it is certainty that causes me not to change.

"He is no wise man who will quit a certainty for an uncertainty."

Samuel Johnson
The Idler, No. 57

Inflexibility

Willful refusal to consider evidence

Inflexibility pertains to will: it is a decision not to consider that we might be wrong. It is a refusal to be convinced by any amount of *evidence against our position, no matter how overwhelming it may be.

Unlike certainty, which is outward looking, inflexibility is a turning inward. That is, my understanding of objective truth does not cause my inflexibility; it is caused by a subjective attitude: my desire to be right. The reason I do not change is that I do not want to change. Since my inflexibility is not based on evidence, even if new evidence surfaces that proves me to be mistaken, I still will not change.

We are inflexible when we refuse to consider a position contrary to our own. We refuse to accept the conclusion of a logical argument even when we see why it must be true. Those scientists were inflexible who refused to look through Galileo's telescope because they did not want to see that heavenly bodies change. Adherents to political parties are often inflexible in their opinions of the candidates or programs of another party. In these cases, inflexibility is not founded upon the objective character of evidence, but on a subjective refusal to consider evidence.

---

of conviction based on overwhelming
willful refusal to consider evidence.

~

*"Do not persist, then, to retain at heart
One sole idea, that the thing is right
Which your mouth utters, and
nought else beside."*

Sophocles
Antigone

ASK YOURSELF:
*Am I more concerned
with defending my position
than with knowing the truth?
Is my refusal to change my
mind a matter of pride?
If so, it is inflexibility
that dominates me.*

Character

The moral quality of a person

In general, character refers to a person's *virtue or lack thereof. Character may be good or bad. It is not something we inherit. Rather it is the product of our free *choices. Our character is the one thing that we really do create.

My character is subject to objective *moral evaluation. It is better or worse according to a standard of moral *excellence that is the same for me and for everyone else. This is because my character is a result of all my free choices concerning matters of moral *importance. If I act bravely in this or that situation, I become more *courageous. If I follow my self-interest and act unfairly, I become more selfish and less just. My character may seem natural, like an inherited trait, but it is actually a product of the choices I make.

Character ranges from good to bad. There are very few of us who are thoroughly good and very few of us who are thoroughly bad. Most of us are somewhere in between. Character types dominated by good moral habits are described by reference to virtues: *just, kind, *honest, brave, temperate, merciful, *wise. Character types dominated by bad moral habits are described by reference to vices: unjust, cruel, dishonest, *cowardly, intemperate, hardhearted, *foolish.

Character is a moral quality, the
is a matter of psychological

ASK YOURSELF:
*Is this quality
a matter of
virtue or vice? Is
the person respon-
sible for this
quality? If so,
it is character.*

*"Character building
begins in our infancy,
and continues until death."*

Eleanor Roosevelt

Personality

The psychological traits of a person

In general, personality refers to a person's inborn tendencies and dispositions. Personality may be pleasant or unpleasant. It is something we inherit. Although we may change our personality to some degree, we do not create it.

My personality is subject to objective study (by psychology, for example), but not really to *moral evaluation. This is because moral evaluation is applicable only to my *choices about matters of moral *importance. My personality is, for the most part, not chosen by me and hence is not morally significant. Temperamentally, I am the way I am. Perhaps, I have a tendency to be shy and serious, or maybe I am naturally outgoing and cheerful. My personality is largely inherited, the sum of my natural tendencies.

The range of personalities is in some sense as large as the number of people, for each of us has a unique personality. Still, it is possible to give examples of personalities dominated by one trait. Thus, some people tend to be quiet, while others are boisterous. Some people are nervous, while others are calm. Some are more energetic than others. One personality is not necessarily better than another, although we may prefer the company of some personalities over others.

---

result of free choices; personality traits, not choice.

"Personality is what you seem to be. Character is what you really are."

Alfred Armand Montapert

⤳

ASK YOURSELF:
Is this quality a matter of psychological tendency? Was the person born with this quality? If so, it is personality.

Chastity

Ordering of sexual activity

Chastity guides sexual impulse according to reason's demands. We are sexual beings by nature. However, unlike other animals, we understand this desire to procreate and its relatedness to the goods of *friendship and family. Chastity guides the sexual impulse according to this understanding.

Chastity involves the awareness of the many dimensions of sexual activity, which is not merely instinctual. I know, in the first place, that it is through sexual intercourse that I was brought into the world. This is the basis for family life and all it entails. I also know that human beings (ourselves included) should be treated with respect, as centers of intelligence and *freedom, not as *pleasure objects. And I know that there is a danger of sexual disease, particularly the deadly AIDS virus. Chastity is the ordering of my sexuality within the context of this *knowledge.

Chastity is a *virtue throughout life. It involves purity before marriage, but it is also required within marriage, where it excludes unfaithfulness and sexual aggression. Although it restricts sexual intercourse, chastity does not forbid all forms of physical contact. Touching is an important means of communication. Comforting another, dancing, and chatting are all compatible with chastity.

Although chastity and prudery are often confused, while prudery is the suspicious

ASK YOURSELF:
*Do I recognize
the goodness and
responsibility
of sexual relations? Do I
reserve them for the twin
goods of love and family?
If so, I am being chaste.*

*"It belongs to chastity that
man may make moderate use of bodily
members in accordance with the judgment
of his reason and the choice of his will."*

Thomas Aquinas
Summa Theologica, II-II, Q. 151, art. 1

Prudery

Scorn for sexual activity

Prudery is the suspicion of sexual activity. Perhaps out of fear of intimate personal relationships or because we think of ourselves as spirits trapped in bodies, we may reject the very idea of our being animals with sexual desires. This unreasonable condemnation of our sexuality is prudery.

Prudery is a fundamentally mistaken view of human sexuality. Whereas chastity orders sexuality within the larger context of human understanding and *moral obligations, prudery is suspicious and scornful of sexuality in itself. If I am a prude, I object not only to sexual activity in this or that context, but to sexual activity generally. It is not just that I have chosen not to be sexually active, but I think that it is wrong for everyone. Moreover, it is not just sexual activity that offends me; I object to all reference to sexuality. This involves an unreasonable rejection of my nature.

Prudery is most obviously the rejection of all sexual activity. But it may also involve the disapproval of all contact between the sexes. To the prude, touching of any sort is suspect. Dancing, for instance, or the comforts of holding hands or hugging are not to be permitted. Even friendly conversation between the sexes might be discouraged, since it might lead to further dangerous involvement.

---

chastity is the reasonable exercise of one's sexuality, rejection of all sexual activity.

〜

"A lady in the west end of the town has carried her prudery so far, as to separate the writings of male and female authors in her library."

Salem Gazette
2 July 1813

ASK YOURSELF:
Do I doubt the goodness of sexual relations? Do I flee from the intimacy and responsibilities of true love and family? If so, I am being a prude.

Choice

Rational motivation

A free choice is the result of deliberation. In order to choose, we must first recognize that there are two or more distinct options. Then we must be able to consider each as, in some way, worth doing. Finally we must be able to come to a decision. Since free choice requires *reason, it is unique to rational beings.

Free choice is a prerequisite for *moral *responsibility. It makes sense to tell me that I should do this or not do that only if I am free to respond. But *freedom of choice does not itself have moral weight, as if my action has moral value because it is freely chosen. The *goodness or badness of my action depends on what I choose to do, not on the fact of choice itself. A bad action is worse if I freely choose it, and a good act is better if I freely choose it.

Some actions seem clearly to be deliberate choices. A student's decision to take a course in twentieth-century literature instead of one in economics is an unforced choice between reasonable alternatives. Moral actions involve free choices. When we *commit ourselves in *friendship to another person, we do so deliberately and reasonably. Immoral actions also imply free choice. To lie is an act of free choice, since I must understand *truth and falsehood and choose to go with falsehood.

By impulse we do things without we guide ourselves and are

~

ASK YOURSELF:
Is this action one I have thought about? Do I know what I am doing? If so, it is based on choice.

"We do not choose the day of our birth nor may we choose the day of our death, yet choice is the sovereign faculty of the mind."

Thornton Wilder
The Eighth Day (1967)

Impulse

Irrational motivation

Acting on impulse is acting without deliberation. There is no real evaluation of the differences between options, consideration of each as worth doing, or final coming to a decision. The action is motivated by *feeling, not *reason. Since impulse does not require rationality, we share this motivation with the other animals.

When I do something impulsively, I do it because of some *pleasure or *pain I am experiencing, or because of some emotional urge I feel, or perhaps because of some instinct. Since such actions do not involve deliberate choice, they are not in themselves *moral actions. However, they are morally significant when I can and should avoid them. Thus, although I feel the urge to lash out at someone when I am angry, I ought to control my anger.

Some actions seem to be clearly based on impulse. When someone yells, "Watch out!" we automatically duck our heads. We do not stop to deliberate about the *wisdom of such a move or what the alternative might be. My sudden outburst of anger when I can't get the drawer unstuck is impulsive. Cheering wildly when the unexpected home run wins the big game, or kicking the dirt when the easy play is botched and the other team scores, is an act of impulse, not deliberate choice.

---

rational consent; by free choice responsible for our actions.

"Moral liberty alone makes man truly master of himself; for the mere impulse of appetite is slavery, while obedience to a law which we prescribe to ourselves is liberty."

Jean-Jacques Rousseau
Social Contract, Bk. 1, ch. 8

ASK YOURSELF:
Is this action one that I just do without thinking? Does it seem just to happen, rather than to be my doing it? If so, it comes from impulse, not choice.

Citizen

Participant in a self-governing community

A citizen is an active member of a political *community. Citizenship is more than a legal status guaranteeing a person a broad range of *rights, such as the right to vote and the right to hold elected office; a true citizen shoulders the *moral *responsibility of communal self-government.

With the responsibilities of active citizenship come many opportunities. Self-governing communities thrive only if their members (you and I) take responsibility for them. If I neglect to contribute my input, I turn over to others the power of decision-making. This is bad, not only because I give up trying to understand what makes the best community, but also because I may have better ideas than others. As a citizen, my opportunities are commensurate with my responsibilities. I get to think about ultimate human questions and contribute to building the best possible community.

The acts of a citizen range from voting to holding public office. Voting is a minimal contribution. A citizen may be involved in various community activities, from helping with local sports programs, to serving on the school board, to working for charity organizations. A citizen may contribute through holding political office. In these activities, a citizen shows active concern for the common good.

Both a citizen and a resident live in a community, in the self-government of the community,

∽

ASK YOURSELF:
Do I have the right to participate in governing this community? Am I actively involved in promoting the common good? If so, I am a citizen.

"The first requisite of a good citizen in this Republic of ours is that he shall be able and willing to pull his own weight."

Theodore Roosevelt
Speech in New York, 11 November 1902

Resident

Inhabitant of a town, state, or country

A resident lives in a political *community, but is not actively involved in it. This may be because the resident is denied full citizen *rights. But even legal citizens sometimes live as mere residents. A resident does not shoulder the *moral *responsibility of communal self-government.

With the mere resident's characteristic refusal of responsibilities come fewer opportunities. As a resident who refuses to be involved in communal self-government, I do not worry about what would be the best social structures and *laws for the community. This seems to be a benefit, since it gives me more time to do what I please. However, my lack of concern for what would benefit the community also deprives me of real opportunities. I do not get to learn what it takes to cooperate with others, nor do I get to participate in creating the kind of community that is best for us all.

There are no specific acts attached to being a resident. A resident embraces the passive role of simply living in a certain area. A resident may take advantage of what the community offers (security, public services, education) but is unwilling to give anything back to the community. Unlike citizenship, there is nothing about being a resident that implies active concern for the common good.

---

but the citizen actively participates
while the resident does not.

"Most people mistake a town for a city, and a townsman for a citizen. They do not know that houses make a town, but citizens a city."

Jean-Jacques Rousseau
Social Contract, Bk. 1, ch. 6, fn.

ASK YOURSELF:
Do I live in this community? Am I unconcerned about and uninvolved in promoting the common good? If so, I am a resident, not a citizen.

Commitment

Reasonable devotion to a goal or person

Commitment is the deliberate *choice to dedicate ourselves to some project, cause, or person. Such a choice is based on a considered *judgment of the worth of the project, cause, or person and an awareness of what we must give up to be so committed.

I am justified in being committed to certain projects, causes, or persons even though there are other worthy projects, causes, and persons. For whatever is good is worth pursuing, and if I am going to make any progress toward a goal or deepen some *friendship, I must be dedicated. So long as my commitment is proportionate to the good at stake, it is legitimate. Trivial things or shallow people are not worthy of lifelong commitments.

The importance of commitment is easily seen. To succeed in math class, we must commit ourselves to study, for the material is hard. If a friendship is going to flourish, loyalty is required from both parties, for no friendship is without its difficult moments. Success in sports requires commitment to learning the game, to training, and to cooperation with teammates. Few athletes can excel without dedicated effort. For our *community to flourish, we must be committed to the common good. This means working through the technical and interpersonal problems that inevitably arise.

Commitment shows a devotion proportionate
fanaticism's devotion is

ASK YOURSELF:
Is my devotion based on thoughtful choice? Does it leave room for appreciating other goods and people? If so, I am committed.

"Characteristic of loyal conduct is fidelity to loyal decisions once made, insofar as later insight does not clearly forbid the continuance of such fidelity."

Josiah Royce
The Philosophy of Loyalty, "Conscience"

Fanaticism

Unreasonable devotion to a goal or person

Fanaticism is the blind dedication to some project, cause, or person. Fanaticism verges on not being a *choice, for the fanatic is so single-minded that he does not deliberate about the worth of the project, cause, or person nor consider the cost of such dedication.

I am not justified in being a fanatic, for no goal or person is so transcendentally important that no other goods matter. If I am fanatical about something, I believe that all other goods can be sacrificed to it. Nothing will turn me from my cause. But this is unreasonable, for I know that there are other things and projects that are intrinsically good and other people who are worth respecting. As a fanatic, I ignore this *knowledge.

The dangers of fanaticism are apparent. If we devote ourselves only to our math homework, we will fail in our other classes, not to mention neglecting our duty to friends, family, and *community. If we are fanatical about what we eat or about being in shape, we are likely to offend others, and we may even end up doing damage to our health. To focus exclusively on the family would be unreasonable, both because we have obligations to larger communities (school, town, nation) and because such a focus ignores one of the strengths and supports of the family — a good community.

---

to the real value of a project, cause, or person;
out of all proportion.

"A fanatic is one who can't change his mind and won't change the subject."

Winston Churchill
News Summaries, 5 July 1954

ASK YOURSELF:
Is my devotion impulsive? Does it rule out the appreciation of other goods and people? If so, I am fanatical.

Community

People who choose to be together

A community is built around some shared vision of what is *good. Communities are not just the results of instinct or *impulse. Rather, they arise out of our rational nature. We form communities because we understand and freely choose to pursue some value or values beyond mere survival.

A community is a new creation; it is a real unity we create over and above ourselves as individuals. In a community, be it a family or a larger social organization, we consciously *commit ourselves to a cooperative pursuit of some good. The better the good we envisage, the better the community. Like *friendship, community involves caring for others for their own sake. In other words, a real community is more than just a way of satisfying mutual self-interest.

Although communities often fulfill material needs, they go beyond this to a sharing of immaterial goods such as *truth, beauty, and *love. Material goods tend to be competitive: the more money or *power I take, the less there is for you. If I take two-thirds of the pie, you can have only one-third. Immaterial goods are cooperative: the more just and generous I am, the better off you are. Since these cooperative goods do not depend on changing circumstances, communities built around such goods tend to be *stable.

A community has a purpose that its members mere conglomeration of individuals

ASK YOURSELF:
Is there a unifying vision for this association? Has the vision been freely chosen? If so, it is a community.

"The state is not determined merely by community of place and by the exchange of mutual protection from harm; there must be a sharing of the good life, in a form at once complete and self-sufficient."

Aristotle
Politics, Bk. 3

18

Group

People who happen to be together

A group need not be built around any shared vision of what is *good. Groups may come into existence in response to instinct or *impulse or the circumstances of time and place. We often form groups because, like all animals, we have a basic need to survive and a desire for *pleasure.

Unlike a community, a group is not a real unity over and above its individuals. We are members of a group quite often due to external factors: where or when we live, the fact that our last names begin with the same letter, or someone else's decision. We tend to be unconsciously influenced by a group, rather than freely forming it around some understood good. Belonging to a group does not imply that we care about the well-being of its members.

Lacking this direct concern for others, groups reflect the needs and pleasures of the moment or merely the circumstances of time and place. Shoppers at Wal-Mart at 2:00 on a Thursday afternoon constitute a group. Sharing a cultural or social background makes a person a member of a group. To the extent that groups find their identity in passing things, their cohesion tends to be transient: when the external reason for the group disappears, the group rapidly disintegrates.

---

recognize and support, whereas a group is a
without any shared vision of the good.

*"A crowd is not company,
and faces are but
a gallery of pictures, and
talk is but a tinkling cymbal,
where there is no love."*

Francis Bacon
"Of Friendship"

ASK YOURSELF:
*Do I just happen
to be part of this
association? Am
I unconcerned
for the other
members? If so,
it is a group.*

19

Confidence

Unconceited belief in ourselves

Confidence is faith that we can and will succeed. It is built on the *knowledge that we have had some success in the past and that there is good reason to think that we will have more success.

Confidence reaches beyond the self to share with others a realm of objective goods. It is clear that confidence is good for me, but it is also good for others. Confidence inspires me to apply myself with good *hope for success. As my talents are perfected, I live a more richly human life. Such a confidence is also essential to being an effective contributor to the *community. If I have a high evaluation of myself and the intention to justify it, I strive to place my talents at the service of others.

Confidence is important in all human activities. We cannot be effective in athletics without appropriate confidence. In order to contribute successfully, we must believe that we can do our part. Effective *leadership requires confidence. If we are to be successful, we must believe that we can make a difference in the direction of our community and the world. *Friendship also requires confidence. Friendship blossoms best between equals, and equality requires that each person bring a high conception of the value of self as well as a high evaluation of the other.

Confidence is based on a true evaluation based on an arbitrary preference

ASK YOURSELF:
*Do I believe in
my worth and
abilities? Is this
belief based on an
accurate assessment
of myself ? If so, I have
proper confidence.*

*"Self-confidence is
the first requisite to
great undertakings."*

Samuel Johnson
Lives of the Poets: Pope (1868)

20

Pride

Conceited belief in ourselves

Pride is faith that whatever we do is a success. It is based on the vain belief that, if we have done it, it must be right. To be proud is to be blind to our imperfections and limitations.

Pride causes me to dwell on myself, ignoring other people and the realm of objective goods. Clearly, my pride hurts others, but it also hurts me. I may act recklessly and so bring harm to the *community, or I may think that contributing to the community is below me. In addition to harming others, my pride is bad for me. Because I have an inflated valuation of myself, I make little effort and refuse to seek the advice of others who know more than I. Thus, I fail to develop my talents.

Pride is damaging to all human activities. We cannot be effective contributors to a sports team if we are proud. Pride both prevents us from getting better (since we think that we are good enough already) and prevents team play (since we think that we deserve to be the center of the action). In government, pride turns *leadership to *tyranny. We consider our way of doing things to be better simply because it is ours. Pride makes *friendship impossible. If one person thinks of himself as better than the other, there can be no truly reciprocal caring.

---

of our talents and achievements; pride is for ourselves over others.

"Pride consists in a man making his personality the only test, instead of making truth the test. It is pride to think that a thing looks ill because it does not look like something characteristic of oneself."

G. K. Chesterton
The Common Man, 254

ASK YOURSELF:
*Do I believe
that I am the best?
Is my belief based
on an inflated
assessment of
myself? If so, I
am full of pride.*

Conscience

Rational standard for choice and judgment

To act according to conscience is to follow *reason's lead. It is true that feelings always accompany conscience (especially bad feelings with a guilty conscience). However, we feel good or bad about what we choose to do or what we have already done because we know the *choice or act to be right or wrong. Perhaps this is why the word *conscience* means, literally, "with *knowledge."

It is always wrong for me to act against my conscience, for to do so is to do what I think to be wrong. This I must never do. However, it is not therefore the case that if I act according to my conscience, my action is necessarily *good. In addition to following my conscience (always doing what I think to be good), I must also inform my conscience (constantly try to find out what really is good). When I act in accordance with an informed conscience, my action is good.

The final arbiter in our free actions is conscience. It is conscience that tells us that murder is wrong. It is conscience that reminds us to help those who are less well off. It is conscience that encourages us to work hard at school, sports, or our job rather than goof off. It is conscience that tells us that we should strive to be better and should help others to be better, too.

Although conscience may seem to be
that it makes on us reveal

ASK YOURSELF:
*Is my action based
on the knowledge
of right and wrong?
Have I tried to under-
stand the best course
of action? If so, I am
following my conscience.*

*"The only obligation which
I have a right to assume
is to do at any time
what I think is right."*

Henry David Thoreau
"Civil Disobedience"

Feelings

Emotional standard for choice and judgment

Feelings sometimes move us to act, but they cannot tell us how we ought to act. When we have certain feelings, we still need to ask whether or not we should follow them. If we do not ask, we will act arbitrarily. This is inconsistent with our demand that others not treat us just as they feel. For the sake of *fairness and *community, both sides must strive to be reasonable.

I cannot know what I should do simply by consulting my feelings, for feelings change, often very rapidly. Sometimes I feel good about myself and others; sometimes I do not. If I just follow my feelings, my actions may be extremely irrational. The question of whether my generous and kind feelings or my selfish and hateful ones should be encouraged and nurtured cannot itself be settled by feeling. Ultimately I know, not just feel, that kindness and compassion are better than persecution and hate.

Were feelings our guides, it is hard to see how any action could be wrong. There would be a kind of blanket defense: "I felt like cheating." "I felt like being lazy in school." "I felt like killing him." "I didn't feel like helping her." Immorality would be only "not doing what I felt like doing." If this is the final arbiter in our actions, there really is no arbiter at all.

---

a kind of feeling, the moral demands that its seat is in reason.

"The Moral Law is not any one instinct or any set of instincts: it is something which makes a kind of tune (the tune we call goodness or right conduct) by directing the instincts."

C. S. Lewis
Mere Christianity, Ch. 2

ASK YOURSELF:
Is my action based on my emotions? Have I neglected deliberation about the best course of action? If so, I am following my feelings, not my conscience.

Courage

Standing fast for good in the face of danger

The courageous person knows the seriousness of the danger that threatens and the importance of the good to be protected. Knowing these two things, the courageous person freely chooses to risk personal well-being for the good at stake.

Like other *virtues, courage grows with use. I become more courageous by doing brave actions. This sounds a bit strange, since it would seem impossible for me to do courageous actions without already being courageous. There is, however, a difference between doing one courageous act and having courage as a *character trait. Anyone might do one courageous act; the courageous person acts courageously as a matter of course.

Perhaps the prime example of courage is risking our life for a good cause: to protect our family or country, to help the oppressed, or to save the innocent. Courage is needed in many other areas of our lives. It takes courage not to bow to peer pressure when it encourages us to do what is wrong. It takes courage to meet the various challenges of our lives, from academics, to setting out on a new job or project, to making the effort to put a stranger at ease. It takes courage to play hard in a sports game when you do not feel well.

The difference between courage and rashness and *justice, whereas rashness

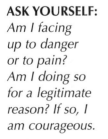

ASK YOURSELF:
*Am I facing
up to danger
or to pain?
Am I doing so
for a legitimate
reason? If so, I
am courageous.*

*Pericles: "The palm of courage will
surely be adjudged most justly to
those who best know the difference
between hardship and pleasure
and yet are never tempted
to shrink from danger."*

Thucydides
Peloponnesian Wars, Bk. 2, 40

Rashness

Courting danger without warrant

The rash person is either unaware of or ignores the seriousness of a danger. Moreover, such a person does not realize the importance of the good at stake. The rash person acts on *impulse more than by conscious, rational *choice.

Like other vices, rashness grows with use. Just as I become more courageous by doing brave actions, so I become more rash by stupidly courting danger. If I make a habit of plunging into dangerous situations without thinking, I take on the *character trait of being rash. Such a habit, once formed, is hard to break. We create our characters by our choices. This is why it is very important to cultivate and practice *virtues such as courage.

Risking our life to save a cat would be rash rather than courageous, since it is clear that a human life is much more valuable than a cat's. It is foolhardy to challenge a gang of six to a fight — despite what we see Clint Eastwood do in the movies. Likewise, it is rash to do a life-endangering stunt just to get attention or make money. It is unreasonable to risk our life for such insignificant goods. Although playing through *pain is courageous, it is rash to play in a sports game with a serious injury that will likely cause permanent damage.

---

is that courage is always guided by *prudence
acts without regard for either.

"That valour which has not prudence for its guide falls under the name of rashness; and the rash man's successful actions are rather owing to his good fortune than to his bravery."

Miguel de Cervantes
Don Quixote, Pt. 2, ch. 28

ASK YOURSELF:
Am I careless of danger or pain? Am I doing so for a cause that cannot be justified by reason? If so, I am rash, not courageous.

Creativity

Inspired ability to make something beautiful

Creativity brings something new and beautiful into the world. This is not just something that did not exist before — it was not even thought of before. Creativity makes use of good technique and guiding rules, but it goes beyond these in creating something original and uniquely beautiful.

If I am creative, there is a spontaneity in my activity that could not have been predicted. The new and unique order that I create in a particular work of art is not just the product of applying the best techniques or following the best artistic examples. It involves a *freedom of invention on my part and a new insight into what is beautiful.

The fine arts are the prime arenas for creativity. The creative painter puts together a unique order of composition, color, and line. The creative musician or composer brings to life musical forms that have not been thought of before. Creativity can also be applied to other areas of our lives. We are creative when we choose — according to our tastes, talents, and circumstances — which goods to emphasize in our lives. Creative insight is at the heart of scientific breakthroughs. Even the invention of new and better ways of producing things involves a kind of creativity.

Skillfulness allows us to make things
us to make beautiful

ASK YOURSELF:
Is this ability oriented toward making something beautiful? Is its critical feature the invention of a unique object? If so, it is creativity.

"Poetic intuition [creativity] can neither be learned nor improved by exercise and discipline, for it depends on a certain natural freedom of the soul and the imaginative faculties."

Jacques Maritain
Creative Intuition in Art and Poetry

Skillfulness

Trained ability to do something well

Skillfulness is a matter of technique. Like creativity, it brings something new into the world, but the thing is not unique; it is a member of a class of things of the same *character and high quality. Skillfulness may be necessary, but it is never sufficient, for making a beautiful thing.

If I am skillful, I am a master of technique rather than spontaneous. I know how to do things in the right way. The more technologically advanced my skill is, the more successful I will be. My skillfulness gives me the *freedom to make something turn out the way I want it to be, but my skillfulness does not in itself involve the creative freedom of invention.

Productivity is most obvious in the fields of technology and business. The latest technology produces more for less and is very efficient. Successful businesses learn how to be more productive than their competitors. Artists also must master the best techniques. The best painter has not only a flair for creating something unique but must be well trained in the techniques of applying paint. The best musician must have mastered the technique of producing notes precise in tone and rhythm in order to express his unique musical forms beautifully.

---

of high quality; creativity inspires and original things.

"Something belongs to art only if even the most thorough knowledge of it does not provide us with the skill to make it."

Immanuel Kant
Critique of Judgment, 43

ASK YOURSELF:
Is this ability oriented toward doing something well? Is its critical feature excellence of technique? If so, it is skillfulness.

27

Criticism

The evaluation of a person's ideas or conduct

Criticism is the *honest appraisal of the value of ideas or actions. When thorough and fair, it addresses strengths and weaknesses. Pursued in the right spirit, it is a positive undertaking whose purpose is to gain an accurate understanding for the sake of growing in *wisdom and *virtue.

Although most of us do not like to be criticized (at least as to the shortcomings of our work), constructive criticism is helpful to us. It makes us aware of what is lacking in our work and thus allows us to improve. If I am never criticized, I may become *self-satisfied and not try to do better. Worse, I may grow comfortable with my *faults. This is also bad for the *community, for my uncorrected ideas and actions will likely harm others. Thus, criticism is a public service.

Criticism helps us in many areas. The best way to improve in sports is to have your coach point out your strengths and weaknesses and show you how to improve. I can become a better writer faster if I have the advantage of someone criticizing my work who knows more than I do. Constructive criticism also helps me become a better human being. I emphasize *constructive,* because unfair criticism can make us bitter and hateful.

Criticism benefits the individual and the condemnation harms both through

ASK YOURSELF:
*Is my judgment
a balanced evaluation
of the quality of a
person's ideas or work?
Is it intended to help
the person do better?
If so, it is criticism.*

*"We invite you to criticize our
institutions without reserve. One is not
insulted by being informed of something
amiss, but rather gets an opportunity for
amendment, if the information is taken
in good part, without resentment."*

Plato
Laws, Bk.1, 635a

Condemnation

The devaluation of a person

Condemnation goes beyond evaluation of an idea or action to a declaration of the worthlessness of a human being. It is never *fair and is a wholly negative *judgment, referring only to weaknesses. Because condemnation is unreasonable, it serves no purpose in our quest for *wisdom and *virtue.

In criticizing others, we must never confuse the wrongdoing and the wrongdoer. The wrongdoing should always be condemned, the wrongdoer never. This is because I can never be absolutely certain of the wrongdoer's intention. Nor can I place a fixed value on any human being so that I could judge an *evil action to have completely depleted the good of that person. Unlike constructive criticism, condemnation is not a service to the one criticized or to the *community.

Examples of condemnation are all around us. We might condemn a person because of his ethnic or social background. We might condemn him for not fitting in with a particular clique. We might refuse even to entertain what he has to say because he is a Republican or a Democrat. Worse, we have recently witnessed "ethnic cleansing" in Bosnia, Rwanda, and Kosovo. These are frightening examples of the power of condemnation to destroy community.

community by calling attention to error and merit; its absolute rejection of the individual.

"Neither hating the man because of his corruption, nor loving the corruption because of the man, we should hate the sin but love the sinner."

Augustine
City of God, Bk. 14, ch. 6

ASK YOURSELF:
Is my judgment a negative evaluation aimed more at the person than at the quality of the person's ideas or work? Is it intended to harm rather than help the person? If so, it is condemnation, not criticism.

Dependency

Reliance on another

Dependency may be a natural fact or may be freely chosen. Animals depend on air to breathe. A child must depend on a caregiver. People within a *community form bonds of mutual dependency.

It is characteristic of dependency that it is generally good for the one who is dependent. Dependency is good for me if it provides something I need to survive or to flourish. Thus, I depend on farmers for food and on teachers for *knowledge. Dependency is demeaning only if my flourishing is prevented by it, either because my free *choice is somehow destroyed by it or because I choose to let others make all my decisions for me when this is not necessary or good for me. My dependency is also good for the one on whom I depend, since that person is doing good by helping me.

Dependency is found throughout nature and in many human relationships. Life on earth depends on warmth, air, and light from the sun. Animals depend on plants and on each other for food. Among human relationships, young children depend on parents for life and nurturing. Students depend on teachers for knowledge and direction. Friends depend on each other for mutual help and comfort. Spouses are mutually dependent. Our democratic and capitalistic culture is a complex network of interdependency.

Dependency is a fact of nature and human subjugation violates human

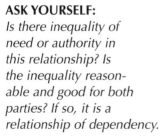

ASK YOURSELF:
Is there inequality of need or authority in this relationship? Is the inequality reasonable and good for both parties? If so, it is a relationship of dependency.

"Heav'n forming each on other to depend,
A master, or a servant, or a friend,
Bids each on other for assistance call,
Till one man's weakness grows
the strength of all."

Alexander Pope
Essay on Man, Epis. 2, l. 249

Subjugation

Absolute domination by another

Unlike dependency, subjugation is unnatural and forced. Human beings are not by nature meant to be subjected to the whims of others. Nor would a sane person choose slavery.

It is characteristic of subjugation that it is not good for the one who is subjugated; rather, it is meant to benefit the one who dominates. It is not good for me to be subjugated, for it takes away my *freedom of *choice. Without freedom of choice, I cannot flourish. I cannot be responsible for my life and for helping others. Although subjugation may seem to be good for the one who dominates, in an important way it is not. The subjugator may benefit in material *wealth; but since subjugation is unjust, the subjugator is acting in a way that destroys his *virtue and thus his chance for real *happiness.

Subjugation, as an unjust relationship of dependency, is found only among human beings who alone have the freedom to be responsible for their actions. Relations of *authority and *obedience may be mutually beneficial; subjugation cannot be. There may be good reasons for a father's authority over his son, but the son is not his father's slave. There may be good reasons for a teacher's authority, but the student is not simply to be brainwashed. In these relationships, as in government, *tyranny destroys *community.

---

relations that is often of great benefit;
relations and is always bad.

"Here was the way to produce a perfect slave. Demand from him unconditional submission, impress upon him a sense of innate inferiority, and instill in him a sense of complete dependence."

Martin Luther King, Jr.
Where Do We Go From Here? (1968)

ASK YOURSELF:
Is there inequality of need or authority in this relationship? Is the inequality arbitrary and bad for both parties? If so, it is a relationship of subjugation.

Discussion

Sharing ideas for the sake of truth

A discussion is an orderly confrontation based on a mutual willingness to learn from one another. It involves the presentation of evidence by each party and then a good-faith attempt of the participants in the discussion to come to agreement.

Discussion presupposes some degree of rational disagreement between us or at least a lack of consensus. If I agreed with you already, we would have nothing to discuss. In a discussion, I do not primarily want to disagree: I want to know the *truth. If I do not think that what you say is true, then I disagree, stating my reasons as clearly as possible and without animosity. The same is true for you: you present me with your reasons. By sharing our ideas freely, we hope to arrive at a deeper truth. In a discussion, disagreement is for the sake of agreement.

Discussions may occur in all sorts of contexts. Scientists come together to discuss the results of their research, hoping to learn from each other. Seminars are designed to encourage discussion among participants, for in such a dialogue new insights and deeper truths may emerge. Among family members, discussions seek mutual understanding of relationships and *responsibilities. Legislative discussions are central to the *political ideal of representative government.

In discussion, we deliberate for the sake
we abandon the mutual pursuit of truth

ASK YOURSELF:
*Am I committed to
the use of reason?
Do I care for the
truth, whether you
say it or I say it?
If so, I am engaging
in a discussion.*

*"Discussion teaches and exercises
at the same time. If I discuss with a
strong mind and a stiff jouster, he
presses on my flanks, prods me right
and left; his ideas launch mine."*

Montaigne
Essays, Bk. 3, ch. 8

Argument

Fighting over ideas for personal victory

An argument (emotional, not rational) is a disorderly confrontation based on an unwillingness to learn from one another. Desire for victory takes precedence over love of *truth, with the result that agreement becomes impossible.

Although they may have rational grounds for disagreement in the first place, all arguments include an element of bad faith — we are not, with all honesty, pursuing the truth together. Rather, in an argument I simply want my position to be the right one and you to agree with me. I am, indeed, looking for agreement, but on my terms, not in terms of objective truth. Instead of my following *reason and leaving passion aside, passion is primary, and reason (if it has a role) works in the service of passion. Quite often, in order to end an argument, we agree to disagree.

Arguments often displace fruitful discussions. Scientists may refuse to share information, accusing each other of stealing ideas. Seminar discussions may degenerate into passionate yelling matches if the participants do not focus on the common work of coming to the truth. Family squabbles may replace open discussions so that *power rules in place of reason. *Politicians may forget their common purpose in promoting *community and turn to character assassination.

---

of coming to the truth; in argument,
because our purpose is to triumph.

"One cool judgment is worth a thousand hasty counsels. The thing to do is to supply light, not heat."

Woodrow Wilson
Speech in Pittsburgh, 22 January 1916

ASK YOURSELF:
Am I committed to victory? Am I willing to use means other than reason to get my way? If so, I am engaging in argument, not discussion.

33

Error

Unintentional wrongdoing

Error is a mistake of the intellect, not of the will. It may occur in any thought process — mathematical, scientific, or *moral. When error occurs in a moral context, it is not in itself blameworthy. It is blameworthy only if we should have known better.

Errors in moral activity can occur because of lack of information or faulty thinking. I may do the wrong thing because I am ignorant of some fact — I do not know that this particular act is wrong. I may do the wrong thing because of a mistake in my thinking — I confuse two closely related ideas. If I do not know what I am doing or that what I am doing is wrong, I cannot be blamed for failing to avoid it. A sign that my mistake is a matter of error and not fault is that I am sorry for the mistake and would have avoided it if I could have.

It is error, not a fault, for me to tell someone what is, in fact, not the *truth when I have been deceived by a reliable source. If my car strikes and kills a child who jumps out from behind a parked van when I am carefully obeying the traffic laws, it is error, not a fault; for I did not have access to the information that the child was there or would run out from behind the van. It is error, not a fault, if I cause many to be sick because I am carrying a disease unknowingly.

Error is an unintended mistake
intentional choice to do what

"An error is not counted as a crime."

Seneca
Hercules Oetaeus, l. 983

Fault

Intentional wrongdoing

Fault is a mistake of the will, not of the intellect. It occurs only in a *moral context; mistakes in mathematics and science are errors, not faults. Fault is when we freely choose to do something we know to be wrong and could avoid doing.

Faults occur only when the reasons for acting are *evil. My wrongdoing is blameworthy (a fault) when it is an action that I could have and should have avoided. I must be able to avoid it: if I cannot avoid it, then it cannot reasonably be said that I chose to do it. I can be blamed only for what I choose to do. If I am coerced or deceived into doing something, it is not my fault. The action must also be something I am obliged to avoid, such as harming the innocent, or manipulating others, or taking what does not belong to me.

It is a fault to lie to those who have a right to be told the *truth, for the good at stake is clear and the deception is intentional. It is a fault to strike and kill a child playing in a residential street when I am speeding. Of course I did not intend to kill the child, but I should not have put the child, other drivers, and myself at risk by speeding. It is a fault if I go to a concert knowing I have an infectious disease, which I could give to others.

---

of the intellect; fault is an
is known to be wrong.

"Crimes are not to be measured by the issue of events, but from the bad intentions of men."

Cicero
Paradoxes of the Stoics,
Paradox 3

ASK YOURSELF:
Is this mistake due to my bad intention? Am I freely choosing what I know to be wrong? If so, it is fault, not just error.

Evidence

Facts that show we are right

Evidence involves objective reasons to believe something is *true. Because evidence is objective, it is the basis for convictions that can be shared by all.

Relying on evidence to support our *judgments about what is true and good builds a *community of shared *knowledge and trust. For if my evidence really is evidence, you will see it, too. When I present objective evidence for my position, I bring with it a willingness to be challenged. You present your objective evidence with the same attitude. Together we contribute to a fund of knowledge that will be there for all. Such a procedure builds mutual trust, since we believe that both of us are seeking the truth rather than the validation of our personal intuitions.

Evidence can be either physical or intelligible. To settle the issue of who came to class today, we rely on our senses to see who is in the room. This is the basic procedure of empirical science, but the sciences often pursue verification with much finer instruments than the naked senses. To settle a question in mathematics, we rely on intelligible proofs based on commonly held axioms. In moral matters, we appeal to the facts of the case and to commonly held norms, such as "Do not intentionally harm the innocent."

Because it is objective and verifiable by others, because it is subjective and

ASK YOURSELF:
Do I justify my position by an appeal to facts? Are these facts available to others, too? If so, I am presenting evidence.

"Let us not underrate the value of a fact; it will one day flower in a truth."

Henry David Thoreau
"Natural History of Massachusetts"

Intuition

Feelings that suggest we are right

Intuition involves the subjective sense that something is *true. Because *feelings are subjective, they cannot guarantee a basis for convictions that can be shared by all.

Relying on personal feelings to support our judgments about what is true and *good fragments the *community of shared *knowledge and trust. If I say that my *judgment about *reality or my decision about a difficult *moral issue is based on my private intuition, you are not likely to take my position seriously. After all, if I claim private intuition as my justification, why should you not do the same? Such a fragmentation of knowledge based on private feeling prevents the establishment of a fund of public knowledge and invites mutual suspicion about the disinterestedness of our efforts.

Some people rely on intuition to settle questions about fashion, food, socializing, and *friendship, and even to solve difficult moral issues. No one would object to our following our feelings about the brand of pants we wear or the flavor of ice cream we order. In many respects, our social life and friendships can be guided by feelings as well as by *reason. But it is clearly not legitimate to decide questions of mathematics or *justice by consulting intuition and feelings; without evidence we risk falling into *error and unfairness.

---

evidence can serve as a basis for public discourse; private, intuition cannot.

"Trust not to thy feeling,
for whatever it be now, it will quickly
be changed into another thing."

Thomas à Kempis
Imitation of Christ, Pt. 1, ch. 13

ASK YOURSELF:
Do I justify my position by an appeal to feelings? Specifically, do I rely on my own feelings? If so, I am presenting my intuition, not evidence.

Excellence

Intrinsic good

Excellence indicates real quality in a thing or person. This quality is objective and can be — and should be — recognized by all people.

What is excellent may or may not be popular. Sometimes excellence is popular, particularly in the realm of high-quality but inexpensive technology. Sometimes excellence is not popular, as in the challenging *moral ideal of putting others first. Nevertheless, the fact that something is not approved by all people, or even by any person, does not make it any less objectively excellent. If John is an excellent guitarist, the fact that you and I do not see this or care does not diminish the quality of his talent. If Susan devotes her life to helping others, the fact that most people do not live this way does not diminish the nobility of her action.

Every kind of thing has its own excellence. An excellent pen writes well, is comfortable to hold, and does not blot. An excellent computer is fast, has a lot of memory, and does not break down. An excellent blueberry bush is healthy and productive. An excellent racehorse runs fast and wins races. An excellent mathematician is intelligent and *logical. An excellent painter is talented, *skillful, and *creative. An excellent friend is kind, generous, *just, and loyal.

Popularity is a matter of collective preference; and exists as an objective standard for

"Every excellence proper to a thing is to be loved in that thing; as in a setter, good scent, and in a boarhound, good speed. And the more proper the excellence the better it is to be loved."

Dante
Convivio, Treatise 1, ch. 12

Popularity

Extrinsic approval

Popularity indicates the desirability of something to people. This desirability is not objective but the subjective preference of a large number of people.

What is popular may or may not be excellent. Sometimes popularity reflects excellence, as when a popular figure in sports, such as Tiger Woods or Pedro Martinez, really is an excellent athlete. Sometimes a popular thing is not excellent, as when an artist is popular for shocking people, not for producing great art. The fact that something is approved by many (or even by all) does not make it objectively *good. If I am a mediocre musician, the fact that I become popular does not make me better. If lying to avoid embarrassment is wrong, the fact that more and more of us start doing it (making it more popular) does not make it a better thing to do.

Since popularity depends on what people like, there is no way to objectify what makes something popular. One brand of shoes may be popular this month, another next month. One TV show may be popular this year, another next year. Movie stars and rock musicians rise and fall in popularity depending on the preferences of their audiences. Who is popular in school depends on who is best able to capture the attention of a significant number of students.

---

excellence is independent of preference
us to recognize and appreciate.

"In questions about good and bad, we ought not to follow the opinion of the many, but the opinion of the one who has understanding."

Plato
Crito 47d

ASK YOURSELF:
Do I and many other people like this thing? Is the question of its objective quality irrelevant? If so, I am judging according to a standard of popularity.

Fairness

Distribution of goods by desert

Fairness is a *moral ideal involving the distribution of goods in a way that takes into account significant differences. If one person deserves more than another because of working harder or risking more, that person should be given more. If one person has more need than another, that person should receive more.

Fairness and equality can coincide. Every person is equally human and therefore should be accorded the *respect due all human beings. This is only fair. But if you risk your life for the *community while I go and hide, fairness demands that you be honored more than I. If I do three-quarters of the work, fairness demands that I receive three-quarters of the pay. Fair distribution is according to the truth about each person's actions. The reasonableness of such distribution is clear to all.

It is fair to give less recognition at a sports banquet to the athletes who cruised and did not produce than to those who worked hard and sacrificed for the team. It is appropriate to honor the wise person whose *wisdom provides order for the community more than the *foolish person whose thoughtless action endangers the common good. More thanks is due to the person who selflessly helps others than to the one who focuses only on himself.

Equality treats everyone the same way; fairness in performance and value, giving

ASK YOURSELF:
Does this treatment reflect differences in merit? Is it based on an accurate valuation of intention, effort, and success? If so, it is a matter of fairness.

"With distributions of honor and property, some possess a fair share and others an unfair share. . . . What is just in distribution should be according to merit of some sort."

Aristotle
Nicomachean Ethics, Bk. 5, chs. 5, 6

Equality

Distribution of goods uniformly

Equality is originally a mathematical concept; applied in a social setting, it means that everyone gets the same. Where people really are equal, equal treatment is due: we are all equal before the *law. But sometimes equality can be unfair: equal *honor paid to all, regardless of talent, effort, or risk, does not seem to be appropriate.

As a political principle, equality is an important ideal, for it underlines the *respect every human being deserves. It is less successful when applied in other arenas. If you have more talent than I, it does not seem fair that I should get the same recognition as you. If Mary is a more intelligent and successful student than Bill, she should get the better grade. Equal distribution for unequal service ignores the truth about each person's actions. The unreasonableness of such distribution is clear to all.

When equality is taken as the most important principle, those members of a team who did not try or care about the team are given the same recognition as those who worked hard for the team and excelled. Every worker is paid the same, regardless of effort and production. The members of a *community who are *foolish and selfish are honored equally with those whose *wisdom and generosity have made the community better.

---

takes into account significant differences
more where more is deserved.

*"There exists also in the human heart
a depraved taste for equality,
which . . . reduces men to prefer
equality in slavery to
inequality with freedom."*

Alexis de Tocqueville
Democracy in America, Vol. 1, ch. 3

ASK YOURSELF:
*Does this treatment
ignore differences in
merit? Is it the same
for all, regardless
of intention, effort,
and success? If so, it
is a matter of equality.*

Faith

Warranted trust

Faith is reasonable trust that something is true even though the *truth cannot be verified. Yet it is an intelligent trust, not an arbitrary one: there are reasons for the belief. Although we tend to think of faith as religious faith, it is actually an essential element in many aspects of our daily lives.

My faith is warranted when two factors are fulfilled: what is proposed for belief is not contradictory or immoral, and the person from whom I hear the proposal is worthy of belief. If the proposal is contradictory, it just does not make sense. If it is immoral, I have no reason to trust the *character of the person making the proposal. However, I have good reasons to trust some *authorities — such as textbook writers, mapmakers, and caring teachers.

Far from being limited to religion, faith is required in virtually every sphere of our lives. We have faith that the laws of physics will not change tomorrow and that our cars will not fall apart when we drive. We have faith in our *friend's profession of loyalty. In addition, faith is required for learning. If we did not believe in facts of history and geography that we have not experienced, we would never study these things. Thus, faith is not some oddity of religion, but a fundamental principle of nearly all human activity.

Both faith and gullibility trust in faith has reasons for this

ASK YOURSELF:
Are there good reasons for my accepting this on faith? Is the authority to be trusted? If so, my assent is based on a justified faith.

"All our historical beliefs, most of our geographical beliefs, many of the beliefs about matters that concern us in daily life, are accepted on the authority of other human beings."

C. S. Lewis
"On Obstinacy in Belief," in The World's Last Night and Other Essays (1960)

Gullibility

Unwarranted trust

Like faith, gullibility is trust that something is *true that cannot be verified. Unlike faith, however, gullibility involves arbitrary trust: there are no good reasons for it. Far from being an essential element in our daily lives, gullibility is a weakness in the individual and a danger to society.

My gullibility is wrong for two reasons. In the first place, it indicates a weakness in my powers of *judgment or, even worse, a lack of care on my part. My weak powers of judgment leave me open to deception and harm. My lack of care is a *moral flaw on my part. In the second place, my gullibility presents a danger to society, either by setting a bad example for others to follow or by encouraging others to take advantage of me.

Gullibility infects our lives in many ways. The uncritical acceptance of what we see on TV, from the advertised benefit of wearing the right sneakers to the supposed *happiness of Hollywood stars, is an act of gullibility. Willingness to follow the crowd, to yield to peer pressure, is also gullibility, for we have no reason to believe that the crowd knows best. Society's tendency to *honor the rich and *famous is another act of gullibility. We must judge accurately between the market (what sells) and *morality (what is right).

---

what cannot be strictly proven, but trust, and gullibility does not.

"The danger to society is that
it should become credulous,
and lose the habit of testing things
and inquiring into them; for then
it must sink back into savagery."

W. K. Clifford
"The Ethics of Belief,"
in Lectures and Essays (1879)

ASK YOURSELF:
Is my willingness
to believe with-
out good warrant?
Is the authority I am
trusting suspect?
If so, I am being
gullible.

Fidelity

Constant devotion

Fidelity is appropriate loyalty to a person or principle. To the extent that people and *moral ideals are *good, they are worthy of *respect. Fidelity is this respect continued over time.

Fidelity requires objectivity. Whether my fidelity is to a person or to an ideal, I am faithful to something other than myself. I show fidelity to a person only when I am devoted to who the person truly is, not to how the person appears in my imagination. I show fidelity to moral ideals when I strive to live in the best possible way rather than simply following my inclinations. My fidelity is good insofar as the person or principle to whom I am faithful is good. It is essential to fidelity that it be guided by *truth and devoted to *goodness.

Consider the appropriateness of fidelity to persons and principles. Fidelity to persons is crucial for *community. Despite fluctuations in our situation, in our friends' moods, and in our own *feelings, fidelity keeps us constant in *friendships. The same is true of larger social units from the family to the nation. Fidelity can also be reasonably paid to ideals such as environmental integrity, democracy, and free enterprise. Even more reasonable and important is constant fidelity to truth and goodness wherever they are found.

Both fidelity and idolatry show constancy of
by objective valuation, whereas idolatry

ASK YOURSELF:
Is my devotion constant? Does it grant proper respect to a person or principle? If so, my devotion is fidelity.

"A faithful and good servant is a real godsend; but truly 'tis a rare bird in the land."

Martin Luther
Tabletalk, 156

44

Idolatry

Blind adoration

Idolatry is unlimited devotion to a thing, person, or principle. Since things and people are limited in *goodness, none is worthy of unlimited devotion. Idolatry treats what is limited as if it were perfect.

Idolatry is subjective distortion of objective *reality. If I set something up as absolute that is not absolute, I embrace falsity. Whether I idolize money or history or a person, I attribute more *goodness to the object than it has. Since the object is unworthy of that degree of my *love, my idolatry is wrong. To worship a thing or a person (imperfect being) as God (perfect being) is to ignore the *truth and to love what is false. Everything that exists is good to some degree and hence worthy of appreciation, but I must match my devotion to the degree of its goodness.

Idolatry may appear wherever good is to be found, in things, persons, or principles. We can idolize things, from money to the products it buys. We can idolize people, from celebrities to athletes. We can even idolize principles. To idolize environmental integrity is to forget the intrinsic importance of each human life. To idolize democracy or free enterprise is to worship an imperfect system. Real truth and goodness can never be loved unduly, but we should not idolize the present stage of our understanding or of our *virtue.

---

devotion, but fidelity's devotion is guided
absolutizes what is imperfect.

*"The great danger for family life,
in the midst of any society whose idols
are pleasure, comfort, and independence,
lies in the fact that people close their hearts
and become selfish."*

Pope John Paul II
*Sermon in Washington, D.C.,
7 October 1979*

ASK YOURSELF:
*Is my devotion
constant? Does it
worship as perfect
that which is
limited? If so,
my devotion
is idolatry.*

45

Forgiveness

Ceasing to hate the wrongdoer

Forgiveness is an internal mental act that does not necessarily imply the external act of pardon. Forgiveness puts aside the desire to hurt the person who has hurt us or a loved one. It presupposes the *knowledge that we really have been wronged and that such wrong-doing ought to be hated. Forgiveness leaves off hating the person.

I could forgive someone in my heart but still think that he ought to be punished. That's because the purpose of *punishment is not to get back at the wrongdoer but to restore *justice in the *community and *virtue in the wrongdoer. Thus, Pope John Paul II forgave Mohamet Ali Agca for the attack upon his life, but still thought it appropriate that he be punished. Forgiveness is the restoration of goodwill toward a wrongdoer.

We are always free to forgive others, whether we insist on their due punishment or not. Since forgiveness is an act of will, we need only will it for it to be done. We can forgive our neighbor for being *rude to us. We can forgive our spouse for harsh words. We can forgive the swindler for cheating us or the bully for beating us up. It is a particular sign of forgiveness to love the offender even while he still hates us. Whether or not the offense is pardoned, forgiveness banishes all resentment and hatred against the offender.

Pardon is the external declaration that an
is the internal act of will that puts

ASK YOURSELF:
Do I see clearly that I have been wronged? Do I refuse to harbor resentment or hatred for the wrongdoer? If so, I forgive the offender.

"A wise man will make haste to forgive, because he knows the true value of time, and will not suffer it to pass away in unnecessary pain."

Samuel Johnson
The Rambler, 24 December 1751

Pardon

Excusing the wrongdoer without punishment

Pardon is an external act that does not necessarily imply the internal act of forgiveness. Pardon puts aside due *punishment for some greater good. It presupposes the knowledge that there has been wrong done and that ordinarily it ought to be punished. Because of special circumstances, the punishment is remitted.

I could pardon an offense done to me but still hate the offender. For hatred is an interior attitude that is not automatically changed just by declaring that the offense will not be punished. Such a state of affairs can even accompany our thoughts on capital punishment: it is possible to oppose the death penalty but still hate the murderer. There can be many motives for a pardon; genuine *love for the offender need not be one of them.

Consider some examples of pardons and the motives behind them. We might pardon an offender because punishment would only harden him, making him more dangerous to society; or perhaps punishment would cast him into despair, rendering him unfit to lead a productive life. We might pardon an offender because our show of *mercy would make a good impression on some person or *group of people. In all these cases, it is perfectly possible to continue to resent or hate the wrongdoer after the pardon is given.

---

offense will not be punished; forgiveness
aside all hatred of the offender.

*"The right of pardoning, viewed
in relation to the criminal,
is the right of mitigating or
entirely remitting his punishment."*

Immanuel Kant
Science of Right, 49

ASK YOURSELF:
*Do I see clearly
that I have been
wronged? Do I refuse
to insist on a due
punishment for the
wrongdoer? If so, I
pardon the offender.*

47

Frankness

Openness of spirit

Frankness is complete *honesty with others. It is based on a high regard for the *truth. Where truth is expected and at issue, we should always give our frank *opinion.

Frankness includes social tact. That is, if I am frank, I know when it is appropriate to voice my honest opinion. I do not seek opportunities to embarrass people, but reserve my frankness for those contexts in which it will be accepted in the right spirit or when it is necessary to guard against injustice. My frankness is meant to benefit the recipient, and, when I employ it tactfully, it does.

Frankness is an ideal of *friendship. Since friendship is at the heart of all real *community, frankness is also an ideal in all coop-erative ventures. It is a sign of close friends that they may speak freely about whatever is on their minds without taking offense. Within a family, there is normally frank exchange of ideas. If peo-ple are involved in a serious project, it is important that they feel free to criticize each other's ideas and accept *criticism. Even on the national level, frank and open discussion of issues is impor-tant. The key to frankness is that it is of benefit to all who are involved in the exchange.

Frankness is an open exchange for bluntness designed to satisfy

ASK YOURSELF:
Is my bluntness meant to pro-mote friendship and truth? Is it likely to be received in the same spirit? If so, it is frankness.

"Candor is proof of both a just frame of mind, and of a good tone of breeding. It is a quality that belongs equally to the honest man and to the gentleman."

James Fenimore Cooper
The American Democrat (1838), Ch. 23

Rudeness

Offensive bluntness

Rudeness is careless insensitivity or intentional affront to others. What is rudely said may or may not be an expression of what is *true, but it always offends others unnecessarily.

Apparent rudeness may be due to a lack of social tact, but real rudeness is always to some degree intentional. Either I neglect to be courteous where I know better (as with elders), or I mean to offend. If I mean to offend, my rudeness is intended both to harm the recipient by embarrassing or belittling him and to benefit me by making me feel superior. I demean the other to make myself feel good.

Rudeness may infect all human relations. We may use the informality natural within the family and among friends as an excuse for rudeness, taking advantage of the willingness of family and *friends to *forgive us. But rudeness undermines close relationships and is counterproductive, causing hurt feelings and lack of trust. The same is true within *community organizations and in *politics on the state and national levels. Rudeness is divisive, producing general distrust and cynicism. In all cases the open expression characteristic of rudeness is meant to harm rather than to benefit the recipient.

the good of both parties; rudeness is
one party by offending the other.

"Discourtesy is not a single vice of the mind, but a product of several — foolish vanity, ignorance of obligation, indolence, stupidity, destruction, contempt of others, jealousy."

Jean de la Bruyère
Caractères (1688), Pt. 11

ASK YOURSELF:
Is my bluntness meant to hurt others and promote my sense of superiority? Is it likely to offend? If so, it is rudeness.

Freedom

Self-directedness

Freedom is taking *responsibility for our own life. Insofar as it is compatible with the common good, people should be allowed to choose freely how they want to live.

Freedom, within the context of mutual *respect, leads to independent and energetic action. This is certainly preferable to forced conformity. It is good for individuals and the *community. If I can choose to become a teacher or a doctor or an entrepreneur rather than being forced into some job, I will be *happier in my work and more likely to succeed. This certainly benefits me, but it also benefits the community. Of course, freedom is not an absolute: if my free action seriously violates the common good, it should not be permitted.

Freedom is a positive force in many areas. In writing a paper for history class, a certain independence in choosing the topic and method aids the learning process. A coach has to give her athletes a degree of freedom to make decisions in a game, for new situations will arise that demand creative solutions. In government, the freedom to vote gives people a stake in their future. In all of these examples, self-discipline and responsibility are required if the freedom is to be fruitful.

Freedom and license must not be confused: is guided by reason and virtue; license

ASK YOURSELF:
Is it my choice?
Am I acting reasonably and responsibly?
If so, my action is the exercise of freedom.

"*Freedom refers to self-determination. . . .*
To the extent that we can determine
for ourselves who we shall be,
we are responsible for our lives."

Germain Grisez and Russell Shaw
Beyond the New Morality, Ch. 1

License

Self-abandonment

License is the throwing off of all *responsibility. It is a carte blanche to do as we feel. As such, it is incompatible with *virtue and destroys *community.

License, as the throwing off of all responsibility, leads to absurd and dangerous action. On the personal level, license leads to *moral chaos. If my actions are based merely on whim or the *impulse of the moment, they are completely unpredictable, even to me. On the social level, license leads to anarchy — the lack of all dedication to the common good. This is obviously bad for the community, but license is also bad for those who exercise it. I strive to be free from responsibility rather than to be free to take charge of my life.

License can cause damage in the very places where freedom enriches. If license rules in choosing topic and method, a history paper might not even remotely relate to history. Athletes cannot succeed in a sport by acting on mere whim, for each sport requires discipline, and team sports demand a high degree of cooperation. If the members of a society ignore all restrictions of *law, that society will not survive. License abandons personal responsibility and so loses the creative energy and fruitfulness of freedom.

---

freedom embraces responsibility and is *choice without restraint.

"None can love freedom heartily
but good men; the rest love
not freedom but license."

John Milton
Tenure of Kings and Magistrates

ASK YOURSELF:
*Is it my choice?
Am I acting without
concern for reason or
responsibility? If so,
my action is the exercise, not of freedom,
but of license.*

51

Friendship

Mutual affection and esteem

Although there are all kinds of friendships, the deepest and most fundamental is centered on a selfless concern for another person. In true friendship, each party cares about the other for that other's own sake. To be a true friend is to put our friend first.

True friends really care about each other's full *happiness. If I am your friend, I want what is best for you. This means that I want to be useful to you and to make life enjoyable for you. But even more, it means that I want you to be *wise and *good, for only then can you be fully happy. Because true friendship is based on a mutual *commitment to help each other grow in *wisdom and *virtue, it tends to last, for these goods cannot be lost owing to changes in fortune.

In true friendship, there is no *envy or jealousy. Friends do not begrudge the fact that one has achieved or been given some good that the other does not have, but they rejoice in each other's success. Nor is friendship exclusive; it naturally gives rise to and nourishes other friendships. Friends are happy that their friends have other friends. If I am a real friend, I would even give up my chance for glory so that my friend might have it. This *commitment to the full happiness of others is the ideal of all human relations.

Fellowship is the enjoyment of
is dedicated to promoting

ASK YOURSELF:
Is this relationship based on mutual concern for full happiness? Does my concern involve wisdom and virtue as well as pleasure and utility? If so, it is friendship.

"Perfect friendship exists between people who are good and are alike with respect to virtue. Such people are good in themselves."

Aristotle
Nicomachean Ethics, Bk. 8, ch. 4

Fellowship

Mutual enjoyment and camaraderie

Fellowship is a necessary and pleasant part of our lives. But, unlike true friendship, fellowship is not necessarily centered on the good of another. It may be centered simply on the *pleasure of entertaining company. Fellowship is compatible with putting ourselves first.

In fellowship, our care for one another is secondary to our desire for enjoyment. Our fellowship need not involve any dedication to promote each other's full *happiness. Perhaps we share a desire for some object or activity, or maybe we just have fun together. There is nothing wrong with such a relationship, but it lacks the deep *commitment characteristic of true friendship. Since fellowship depends on mutual enjoyment, it may not last beyond our first disagreement.

Although fellowship falls short of the full mutual commitment characteristic of true friendship, it is an important ingredient in social relations. It makes interacting with others easier and more pleasant. Clubs, sports teams, organizations, and businesses all benefit from the cultivation of fellowship. Fellowship supports a spirit of cooperation, contributing to the efficiency and enjoyment of such groups. In addition to being *useful and pleasant, fellowship may eventually develop into true friendship.

---

human relations; true friendship
full human happiness.

"In Fellowship is all my affiance;
We have in the world so many a day
Been such good friends in sport and play."

Everyman
Medieval Morality Play

ASK YOURSELF:
Is this relationship based on mutual usefulness or enjoyment? Does it fall short of a mutual concern for wisdom and virtue? If so, it is fellowship, not true friendship.

53

Genius

Extraordinary intelligence or creativity

Genius is a rare gift. It is the talent of seeing things in a fresh way and the *creative ability to bring into being new instances of beauty or new ways of looking at the world.

A work of genius is often difficult to appreciate fully, not because it is disordered, but because the order is new and subtly complex. This is true both of intellectual breakthroughs and artistic creations. Because Einstein's genius transcended the scientific *knowledge of his day, his insights were difficult to grasp. Likewise, a work of artistic genius is a well of intelligible and sensual delight: at first I may find it strange, but the more I read, hear, or see it, the more I appreciate its beauty.

The genius of Mozart or Picasso or Shakespeare requires some study and time to appreciate. What makes these so successful artistically is not their superior knowledge or their superior *moral *character but, rather, their ability to create works of art that are original, integrated, and unified. The intellectual genius of Aristotle or Aquinas or Einstein provides a continual challenge to our understanding. They bring to life an exceptional and compelling vision of *reality, and, like artistic masterpieces, their works bear visiting and revisiting.

Eccentricity introduces something new;
a unique work harmoniously

ASK YOURSELF:
Is this intellectual or creative work impressive because of its brilliant truth or beauty? Is it exceptional for its unique integration of elements into an ordered whole? If so, it is the product of genius.

"Genius is a talent for producing that for which no definite rule can be given. However, its products must at the same time be models, that is, exemplary."

Immanuel Kant
Critique of Judgment, 46

Eccentricity

Extraordinary idiosyncrasy or quirkiness

Eccentricity is open to anyone. To be eccentric, we need only to be *self-absorbed and let whatever comes out come out. Eccentricity does not require talent or *creative ability.

An eccentric work can be difficult to appreciate merely because it is narrow and quirky. Often it is simply disordered. Such eccentricity in intellectual arenas soon fails to bear fruit, but it is often successful in the arts. An eccentric piece of writing may be hard to grasp because it is badly written or *obscure. If I do not appreciate the musical form of an eccentric work of music, the reason may be that there is none. Eccentric works often do not reward multiple experiences of them.

The eccentricities of some artists are striking more because they are quirky than because they are masterful creations of ordered harmony. Much of modern art is a product of the effort to be eccentric — to do something that has never been done or to shock people in new and bizarre ways. In many cases, the novelty is a matter of new ideas rather than beauty. Intellectual eccentrics can be fun to read, but since they are so idiosyncratic, it is difficult for them or others to build on their ideas. Like the products of artistic eccentrics, their works do not bear repeated visits.

---

genius does this and more by creating ordered in a unified whole.

"Anarchism adjures us to be bold creative artists, and care for no laws or limits. But it is impossible to be an artist and not care for laws and limits. Art is limitation; the essence of every picture is the frame."

G. K. Chesterton
Orthodoxy, Ch. 3

ASK YOURSELF:
Is this intellectual or creative work impressive because it is new or exciting? Is its appeal based primarily on its being radically different? If so, it is the product of eccentricity.

Goodness

What is desired for its own sake

Although goodness has many meanings, the most basic meaning is that it is something worthy in itself. It is not valued just as a way to get some other thing. It is worth having even if it does not lead to anything else.

What is good in itself cannot be considered merely a means to some other thing or just an aspect of something else. I cannot account for the particular worthiness of such a good by pointing to something to which it leads, as penicillin leads to health. Nor can such a good be explained by reference to other goods, as a triangle can be explained by straight lines. I see immediately that things good in themselves can and should be recognized as good by everyone. Such goods are the heart of *happiness and foundational for real *community.

*Knowledge, *friendship, and beauty are good in themselves. Although certain kinds of knowledge are desired because they lead to something else, we can say in general that it is good to know and bad to be ignorant. Even to ask whether knowledge is good presupposes the desirability of finding out. *Friendship is good, particularly if we have in mind friendship of mutual devotion. Nor is there anyone who does not appreciate beauty, at least of some kind.

What is good is valued
useful is valued for

*Do I desire this
thing? Is it desirable
in itself rather than
for the sake of
something else?
If so, it is something good.*

"*Since all things are sought on
account of the good, it is the
good itself, not the other things,
which is desired by everyone.*"

Boethius
*Consolation of Philosophy,
Bk. 3, prose 10*

Usefulness

What is desired for something else's sake

What is useful is valued because it leads to something else. It may also be good in itself, but the reason it is desired is to achieve some other good that is desired more. Thus, the useful cannot be the most essential meaning of *good.*

Unlike something that is good in itself, a useful thing does not have irreducible value. Since I desire it as a means to some other good, the useful is replaceable. What really matters to me is that I can get that other good; it matters little what I use to get it. Any instance of the useful thing will serve. Indeed, if I find a second thing more useful, it makes sense for me to abandon the first. Because the usefulness of such things may change with time and place, they are not intrinsic elements in *happiness nor foundational for real *community.

Many things are useful. Pens are useful for writing, and writing, for communicating ideas. Maps are useful for telling us how to get somewhere, and cars, for getting there. Some things are useful and good in themselves. Knowledge of history is useful for passing your exam, but it is also good to know what really happened. A beautiful painting is useful for paying the bills when the artist sells it, but it is also good just because it is beautiful.

---

for its own sake; what is
what it can bring.

"Though the useful
is not always good,
the good is always
useful."

John Henry Newman
The Idea of the University,
Discourse 7, sect. 5

ASK YOURSELF:
Do I desire this
thing? Is it
desirable as a
means to something
else that is desired
more? If so, it is
something useful.

57

Gratitude

Giving thanks for good received

Gratitude is being thankful for the gift of something *good. Gratitude is a *choice we make, not an automatic result of giving and receiving. It is a free act of the will, given easily to another.

Gratitude may appear to be a sign of subservience and hence weakness, but it is not. It is simply the appropriate response to good received. There is nothing demeaning in this. No one forces me to be grateful. Since I seek what is good, it makes sense to be thankful when I am given it. It is my free *moral act. I know the importance of doing good and the effort it takes. Given these two things, it is reasonable for me to express my appreciation to someone who has done good to me. It is true that sometimes gratitude seems to well up spontaneously; but even here, it is in the context of my knowing that I have received a good gift.

Although there is no case of indebtedness that automatically causes gratitude, we have, I believe, all experienced gratitude. Perhaps we have had the good fortune to escape what seemed to us an inevitable calamity. Maybe it has been a case where we were *forgiven although we knew we did not deserve it. Perhaps, we have had the experience of being grateful for being loved or for the simple wonder of existing at all.

Gratitude is reasonable and freely given thanks of being obligated to someone

ASK YOURSELF:
Am I obligated
to another for good
I have received? Do I
cheerfully acknowledge
my debt and respond
with proper honor and
respect? If so, I am grateful.

"A hundred times every day I remind myself that my inner and outer lives are based on the labors of other men, living and dead, and that I must exert myself in order to give in the same measure as I have received and am still receiving."

Albert Einstein
The World As I See It (1931)

58

Indebtedness

Owing thanks for good received

Indebtedness is being beholden to another for the gift of something good. Indebtedness is a fact, not a *choice one makes. If there is a relationship of giving and receiving, there is indebtedness.

Indebtedness suggests that I owe something to another. This is a kind of subservience and implies a certain weakness: something of mine is owed by right to another. If I pay my debt, I'll lose something I now have. The very fact of someone giving me something forces me into indebtedness. However, my indebtedness does not imply gratitude on my part. On the contrary, I may see the subservience it suggests as demeaning and become resentful. This resentment, of course, does not automatically follow indebtedness any more than gratitude does; but the gratitude is more reasonable, for one should return *good for good.

It is easy to think of ways in which we are indebted. We are indebted to our parents for giving us life. We are indebted to those who nurtured us so that we might grow to *maturity. We are indebted to those who have given of their time and energy to educate us. We are indebted to those through whose vigilance and thoughtful *prudence we live in a *free society with a flourishing economy and *law-based *justice system.

---

for a good received; indebtedness is the fact
for good we have received.

"A debt and gratitude are
different things. He who discharges
a debt in money ceases to possess
what he has paid. In gratitude,
what I pay I keep, and what I keep
I pay by the very act of keeping."

Cicero
Pro Placio, Ch. 28, sec. 68

ASK YOURSELF:
*Have I received
good from
another? Have I
failed to repay
that good in
kind? If so, I
am indebted.*

Greatness

Worthiness of acclaim

A person who is great is worthy of note, even if not well known. The worthiness comes from some real *excellence in the person; it does not depend on the *opinion of other people. Strictly speaking, fame can add nothing to greatness. Since greatness inheres in the person, it cannot be lost or taken away.

Greatness should be acknowledged by others. If we judge correctly and discriminate between the really *good and what is only apparently good, then we will give *honor where honor is due. Those with real greatness should also be famous. If those with real talent, those with substantial accomplishments, and those with real *virtue were famous, we would have good models to emulate and a stronger *community.

People who care selflessly for the poor and the sick are great, but few are famous (Mother Teresa was an exception). Parents who bring up their children well amid the difficult challenges of the modern world are certainly great, but they live without fame. Many great thinkers in the world are not famous: *wisdom does not sell. Artists and musicians with great talent go unrecognized, because few people care or know enough about art to appreciate their *skill and their *genius.

Fame is the mere fact of name recognition; of the one who is great, not

⌣

ASK YOURSELF:
Is this characteristic based on real excellence? Is the excellence intrinsic, so that it can not be taken away? If so, the characteristic is greatness.

"Greatness isn't determined by how many people know you; it's determined by service to other people."

Oprah Winfrey
In "An Intimate Talk with Oprah," Essence, August 1987

Fame

Widespread acclaim

A person who is famous is well known, even if not worthy of note. Fame depends on other people's *opinions, not on any intrinsic worth of the famous person. Although greatness may accompany fame, there is no necessary connection between the two. Since fame is extrinsic, it can easily be lost or taken away.

The mere fact of being famous does not call for acknowledgment by others; in fact, in many cases fame can lead us astray. The glamour of a famous person can fool us into thinking that he is worthy of praise and emulation. But if there is no real greatness, we end up worshiping mere *popularity and lose the ability to *judge with discrimination. Where there is no real greatness, no *honor should be paid.

Many movie stars and contemporary musicians are famous even though they have little talent. In fact, fame and meager talent often are found together, for average talent and average creative art are easier for people to catch on to. The bestselling self-help books are, in many cases, shallow. *Politicians often get elected because brilliant media campaigns give them name recognition rather than because they have good ideas, are outstanding *leaders, or are particularly *virtuous.

true greatness is rooted in the intrinsic worth in the opinion of the crowd.

"Be more concerned with your character than your reputation. Your character is what you really are, while your reputation is merely what others think you are."

John Wooden
UCLA basketball coach

ASK YOURSELF:
Is this characteristic based on popularity? Is this popularity extrinsic, so that it can be taken away? If so, the characteristic is fame, not greatness.

61

Happiness

Human fulfillment

Happiness is more than just bodily pleasure or psychological satisfaction: it is the fulfillment of every aspect of our being. We desire to be pleased and satisfied, but unlike the other animals, we seek meaning; our very question "What is happiness?" is a case in point. Living a life of meaningful activity, guided by intelligence and free will, is the heart of human happiness.

Happiness arises primarily from something I do, not from something I receive. It is not a mere effect in me of some external cause, like warmth in the pavement caused by the sun. In the first place, happiness requires self-awareness: I cannot be happy if I do not know that I am happy. In the second place, if happiness is to be mine, I must in some sense be *responsible for it. My purposeful activity must form the heart of my happiness.

*Truth, *goodness, and beauty are the objects of such meaningful activity. We find meaning in seeking and coming to know the truth about the world around us, ourselves, and our place in the world. We find meaning in living lives of *moral goodness, growing in *virtue, and helping others to do the same through our *friendships, families, and *communities. We find meaning in appreciating the beauty of nature and art and in creating beautiful things.

Pleasure is something we receive from an we do — the meaningful activities

"Happiness is
a state made perfect
by the union of
all good things."

Boethius
*The Consolation of
Philosophy, Bk. 3*

Pleasure

Satisfaction or excitement

Although we speak of many kinds of pleasure (sensual, mental, even *moral), pleasure is most fundamentally a bodily satisfaction. Certainly, seeking pleasure and avoiding *pain are natural to us, but they are not distinctive human characteristics. Satisfaction and excitement are desired by all animals. Experiencing pleasure and pain does not require intelligence or free will.

Pleasure is not so much something I do as something I receive. Unlike happiness, pleasure may be a mere effect in me of some external cause, such as the pleasure of lying in the sun or the pleasant feeling induced by drinking alcohol. Experiencing pleasure does not require self-awareness or purposeful activity. All animals respond to pleasure and pain, but clearly not all are self-aware or consciously *responsible for their activity.

Pleasure is indeed an ingredient in human happiness: the *wise, *virtuous person is happier if not stricken with physical and emotional pain. But not all pleasures promote happiness: the pleasure of taking addictive drugs destroys a person's ability to make meaningful *choices and hence to be happy. Nor are all pains incompatible with happiness: the happiness of playing a sport includes the pain of getting in shape. Hence happiness is not identical with pleasure.

object or an action; happiness is something of thinking, choosing, and creating.

"Pleasures are insubstantial and unreliable; even if they don't do one any harm, they're fleeting in character. Look around for some enduring good instead."

Seneca
Letters to Lucilius, 27

ASK YOURSELF:
Do I seek only sensual satisfaction? Do I think that meaning is irrelevant? If so, I am pursuing pleasure.

Honesty

Complete adherence to truth and justice

To be honest is always to be open and *fair. It is to act without guile or pretense. The honest person speaks the *truth and acts justly, not because it is advantageous to do so, but simply because it is right to do so.

It is immediately evident that my honesty is good for others, for I will always tell them the truth and treat them fairly. If we were all honest, many *laws would be unnecessary. However, it is also true that my honesty is good for me, even if my honesty brings me fewer material goods (money, *power, *fame) than dishonesty would. By preferring the greater and more lasting goods — such as *knowledge and *virtue — over lesser and more transient material goods, I live a more human and hence happier life right now.

The honest person is always forthright and open in dealing with other people. She neither hides anything that the other person ought to know, nor fails to honor her promises, even when fulfilling them will bring her harm. The honest person is guided by fairness in all her actions. Not only would the honest person not cheat others; she would even correct a mistake made by a merchant in her favor. Honesty nurtures mutual trust, without which there can be no real *community.

To be honest is to act with openness
to allow ourselves to be

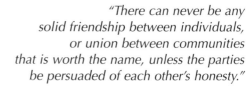

ASK YOURSELF:
*Am I committed
to truth and fair-
ness? Am I willing
to follow these even
if doing so may not
be to my advantage?
If so, I am honest.*

*"There can never be any
solid friendship between individuals,
or union between communities
that is worth the name, unless the parties
be persuaded of each other's honesty."*

Thucydides
Peloponnesian War, Bk. 3, 10

Naïveté

Inability to recognize lies and injustice

It is often said that someone is honest to a fault. Although this cannot literally be the case, it is possible to leave ourselves and those for whom we have *responsibility open to being cheated without necessity. This is to be naïve.

It is evident that my naïveté will likely lead to bad consequences for me, for there are people out there who are looking for someone to swindle. Not only does being naïve lead to the loss of material goods; it is also bad for my *character, for I fail to *judge prudently the situations in which I find myself and the motives of those I meet. Being naïve is also bad for others, since it permits them to treat me unfairly. It is not that my naïveté excuses their behavior, but my *prudence could remove a temptation for them.

The naïve person assumes that all other people are trustworthy, with the result that he is not able to recognize the swindler who wishes to cheat him or the criminal who is dangerous. It would be naïve, for example, to believe that the salesman on the phone really has your best interests in mind or that the "friendly" stranger in the blind alley can be trusted. *Openness is essential for real *community, but it is not good to put yourself or another at risk unneccesarily. Blind trust is no *virtue.

---

and fairness; to be naïve is foolishly manipulated and deceived.

"Of all the forms of innocence, mere ignorance is the least admirable."

Arthur Wing Pinero
The Second Mrs. Tanqueray, Act 2

ASK YOURSELF:
Am I unable to recognize deceit and danger when I meet them? Am I willing to trust others without warrant and to follow them wherever they lead? If so, I am naïve.

Honor

Acclaim paid to another for good done

Real honor assumes that the actions of the person honored are worthy of *respect and imitation. The justification for the acclaim is based on something objective. Although honor is a form of external approval and not itself a *virtue, it is intimately tied to virtue. It is the response one should have to the virtuous person. Not to honor such a person would be wrong.

It is worthwhile for me to seek to do deeds worthy of honor. This is not because of possible external rewards (*fame and fortune), but because in striving to be worthy of honor, I benefit the *community and make myself a better person. The community benefits in two ways: directly, because helpful actions are performed; indirectly, because there is a good model to be imitated. I benefit because I live a life more in accord with *reason and virtue.

Honor is due in a number of cases. We should honor those whose selfless actions have helped us, especially our parents. We should also honor those who serve the community — teachers, *leaders, public officials. (We should not honor those who misuse their positions of *authority, since they abuse the trust of those they should be serving.) We should honor accomplishments, whether academic, athletic, or artistic, for they are the results of dedication.

What makes honor good is the real virtue
flattery evil is the self-serving

ASK YOURSELF:
Is this person worthy of respect? Is my acclaim paid in celebration of the goodness of this person? If so, my acclaim is honor.

"Worthy of honor is he who does no injustice, and worthy of more than twofold honor is he who not only does no injustice himself, but hinders others from doing any."

Plato
Laws, Bk. 5, 730b

Flattery

Acclaim paid to another to get something

Flattery does not require that the actions of the person flattered be worthy of *respect and imitation. No justification for the acclaim is needed, for it is based on whatever the subjective aim of the flatterer happens to be. The acclaim is a means to an end, a way for the flatterer to gain something he wants. Flattery has no necessary connection with any real good in the person being flattered.

It is not worthwhile for me to seek to be flattered, for flattery is hollow and deceptive. It is not based in any real merit in me but in the flatterer's desire for gain. Such false acclaim is fleeting: as soon as the flatterer gets what he wants, his attention will end. For me to encourage flattery is bad for the *community and bad for me. Those who flatter me are self-seeking, using me to gain what they want. I am hurt, since I seek *pleasure, not *virtue.

Examples of flattery are not hard to find. The student who ingratiates himself with his teacher to get a good grade is a flatterer. So is the child who butters up Mom or Dad to get her way. The ambitious politician fawning on those with money to get him elected is a flatterer. So are those who falsely praise a government official in hope of influence. When we pretend to honor the rich and *famous so that we can look good or get ahead, we are guilty of flattery.

in the one who is honored; what makes intentions of the flatterer.

"The aim of flattery is to soothe and encourage us by assuring us of the truth of an opinion we have already formed about ourselves."

Edith Sitwell
Quoted by Elizabeth Salter in
The Last Years of a Rebel (1976)

ASK YOURSELF:
Is it irrelevant whether this person is worthy of respect? Is my acclaim paid in the hope of getting something for myself? If so, my acclaim is flattery, not honor.

Hope

The will that what is good might be

Hope involves the conviction that, despite appearances to the contrary, *truth and *goodness will prevail. To hope is to *commit ourselves to the betterment of ourselves and the world.

Hope is creative. It involves my vision of and expectation for a good future and my readiness to do what I can to bring about such a future. Although I can wish for anything, I hope only for what is possible. My hope looks to the future, but it is rooted in reality as it is. In this sense, hope is realistic. Hope is idealistic in that it envisions the perfection of that reality. Thus, hope is the product of a conscious *choice to believe what *reason says may and should come true.

What we hope for, we are also willing to work for, if it is in our power. If we hope to get a good grade in a course, we try to bring about such a reality. If we hope to find someone to love, we try to make ourselves lovable by loving. We hope to be more *just, generous, and *forgiving, and so we work to be better human beings. We hope for *peace on earth and try, in our own small ways, to make such peace a reality. We hope that *love will triumph over death, not because of some fantasy, but because we know the reality and power of love.

We may wish for anything at all, but we know to be really

"Hope arouses,
as nothing else can arouse,
a passion for the possible."

William Sloane Coffin, Jr.
Once to Every Man (1977)

Wish

The desire that what one wants might be

Wish involves the fancy that, despite appearances to the contrary, our desire will be satisfied. To wish is to invoke fortune to bring us what we want, even when what we want is not *good.

Wish is imaginative. In order to wish for something, I need not envisage or really expect the wish to come true, nor need I be inclined to dedicate myself to make my wish a reality. My wish has no particular bond with reality as it is, but feeds on fantasy. I can wish for anything that I can imagine, even what is impossible. Wishing is like dreaming: it is not confined to reality as it is, nor is there any good reason to believe that my wish will come true.

When we wish for something, unlike when we hope for something, we are not necessarily willing to work for it. We wish for all sorts of unattainable and frivolous things. We wish we could win five gold medals in the Olympics. We wish we would win six million dollars in the lottery. We wish we were famous like our favorite rock star or movie actor. We may even, at times, wish to be somebody else whose looks or talents appeal to us. Wishing is easy and makes no demands on us either to choose *truth over fantasy or to choose good over *evil.

we hope for what, in our heart of hearts, good and really possible.

"I've often wish'd that I had clear
For life, six hundred pounds a year;
A handsome house to lodge a friend;
A river at my garden's end;
A terrace walk, and half a rood
Of land set out to plant a wood."

Jonathan Swift
Imitation of Horace, Bk. 2, sat. 6

ASK YOURSELF:
*Do I desire to receive what I want?
Do I fantasize
that this might just
appear through no
effort of my own?
If so, I wish.*

Humility

Proper understanding of our worth

Humility involves admitting the *truth about ourselves. We do not know everything; we do not do everything right. Such an admission is prerequisite for growth in understanding and in *virtue, for we seek something only if we know we do not have it.

Humility is necessary for living virtuously and productively with others. If I think I have all the answers, I am unwilling to entertain the possibility that I could be wrong or could learn from others. Not only does humility fit me for honest communication and cooperation with others; it is also grounds for *hope. For my forthright recognition of my limitations implies the *knowledge of the ideals of *wisdom and *goodness and my capacity to grow in them.

Humility is necessary in many areas of our lives. We should be humble before a person of superior knowledge, whether that person is a teacher, a coach, or a parent. Such humility is good for these human relations and the social order in general, but it is also good for ourselves, since only by being humble can we learn. We should be humble about our achievements, for we have never done as much as we could have done, and there are many other equally worthy areas of success that we have not attempted. Again, truth is critical to proper humility.

Humility is the true evaluation of ourselves
the unreasonable identification of

ASK YOURSELF:
*Do I understand
myself to be imperfect?
Do I see myself as
needing help and so
believe that I can and
should improve? If so, I
am guided by humility.*

*"The foundation of humility is the truth.
The humble man sees himself as he is.
If his depreciation of himself
were untrue, it would not
be praiseworthy."*

Henry Fairlie
The Seven Deadly Sins Today

Self-contempt

Unwarranted degrading of our worth

Self-contempt is the confused and unjustified rejection of ourselves. For it is clear that we know some things and that we do some good. Self-contempt prevents us from growing in *wisdom and *virtue, for we do not seek to perfect what we think is worthless.

Self-contempt makes living virtuously and productively with others impossible. If I think I am worthless, I will make no effort to improve, nor will I think I have anything worthwhile to offer the *community. Not only does self-contempt cut me off from honest communication and cooperation with others; it also can lead me to despair. If I think I am worthless, I may give up on life, abandoning *hope that anyone could care about me and my *happiness.

We may feel self-contempt in any number of situations, but in none of them is it warranted. Self-contempt may be our reaction to failure, whether academic, romantic, or *moral. While we should always try our best to succeed, we must keep in mind our limitations. No one can succeed in every enterprise; and when we fail in a particular effort, we should remember that there will be other opportunities and that other kinds of worthwhile activities beckon us. What is true for our judgment of another should be true for our judgment of ourselves: hate the sin, but love the sinner.

---

with all our limitations; self-contempt is our value with our imperfections.

"The man who thinks himself worthy of less than he is really worthy of is unduly humble, whether his deserts be great or moderate, or his deserts be small but his claims yet smaller."

Aristotle
Nicomachean Ethics, Bk. 4, ch. 3

ASK YOURSELF:
Do I consider myself to be worthless? Do I see myself as so beyond help that I despair of improvement? If so, I am driven by self-contempt, not guided by humility.

71

Impartiality

Unwillingness to judge people unfairly

Impartiality is a fundamental principle of ethics. It means that no favoritism should enter into our decision-making. We must be open to the *good of all. Impartiality requires a positive effort, for it is easy for us to favor ourselves or those close to us.

My impartiality benefits others and myself. To treat other people *fairly is to allow each person the same opportunity I desire for myself and for my closest *friends and relations. No one group is given arbitrary advantage over any other. Thus, my unbiased actions support the development of *community. Not only is impartiality good for my community; it is also good for me. For by being open to all, I can discover resources of good that bias would have hidden.

The need for impartiality comes up almost every day. Parents should be impartial in their treatment of their children; one child should not be arbitrarily favored over another. Teachers should be impartial in administering fair grades. Being a good coach of a sports team requires impartiality; if the coach shows favoritism, team spirit and cooperation will suffer. In every case, arbitrary favoritism for one party over another destroys the *fairness and often the success of the enterprise.

Both impartiality and indifference treat
equal respect, whereas indifference

*"It is an abomination
of the gods to show partiality.
Look upon him who is known to thee
like him who is unknown to thee."*

Ancient Egyptian Proverb

Indifference

Unwillingness to judge actions or ideas

Impartiality can easily slip into indifference. Indifference is a passive refusal to be engaged in the lives and ideas of others. There is no positive effort; rather indifference is a lack of concern and thoughtfulness. We just do not care.

My indifference, like my impartiality, shows lack of preference and is fair to this degree. However, although my indifference may not give others an advantage over you, it certainly cannot be said to help you. If I am indifferent, I have no more concern for *justice and compassion than for Pepsi and chips. That's why indifference undermines *community. Indifference is also bad for me: if I make no effort, it is not possible for me to learn from others or become *friends with them.

Indifference concerning indifferent things is perfectly fine. Why should we care what color shirts people wear or what kind of soda they drink? But where truth or morally significant actions come into play, it is a different story. What if the issue is other people's having enough to eat or being treated with justice and compassion? When we are indifferent to these things and ignore the humanity of others, we cripple our own humanity and risk sinking to the level of irrational beasts.

---

all equally; but impartiality treats all with
treats all with equal disdain.

"The opposite of love is not hate, it's indifference. The opposite of art is not ugliness, it's indifference. . . . And the opposite of life is not death, it's indifference."

Elie Wiesel
US News & World Report,
27 October 1986

ASK YOURSELF:
Am I showing lack of preference because it's too much trouble to decide or because I do not care? Am I ignoring the well-being of others? If so, I am being indifferent, not impartial.

Importance

Intellectual or moral significance

What is important is known to be worthwhile. It is *reason, not emotion, that measures importance. This means that importance is not just a matter of personal preference but can be explained by reference to objective criteria accessible to all.

In itself, what is important has no direct connection with excitement. I *judge importance, but I feel excitement. This does not mean, however, that what is important cannot be exciting. Ultimately, what is important is exciting because it instills a deep *joy. To know what is *true and *good is to find life full of significance, and a meaningful life is exciting to live. In contrast, a world filled with sensual excitements but void of meaning would be very dull.

There are many examples of things important but not exciting. It is not exciting to learn the basics of grammar and arithmetic, but they are extremely important as foundations for communication and science. Eating nutritious food may not be exciting, but it is important for our health. It may not be exciting to learn the principles of *logic or *morality, but they are essential if we are to lead lives guided by reason rather than irrational *impulse. *Chastity and *peace may not be as exciting as pornography and gratuitous violence, but they are critically important for life in a *community.

What is important is judged by exciting is felt by the senses

ASK YOURSELF:
Is this thing something I understand to be good? Would I expect others to count it as good? If so, it is something important.

"It is not so important to be serious as it is to be serious about the important things."

Robert M. Hutchins
University of Chicago,
Quote, 3 August 1958

Excitement

Sensual or emotional stimulation

What is exciting is felt to be worthy of attention. It is emotion, not *reason, that measures excitement. Excitement is not so much explained as experienced. Because experiences are always particular, the criteria for excitement are subjective.

I may find something exciting, but that does not mean it is important. Likewise, if I find something boring, this does not mean that it is unimportant. Boredom is more an attitude or *feeling in me than an indicator of qualities in things around me. To *judge things by my feelings rather than by reason is to be at the beck and call of circumstances. For what brings me emotional and sensual pleasure can change from moment to moment against my will.

There are many causes of excitement — some important, some unimportant, and some bad. We can be excited by ideas or by impressive achievements in sports or music. We can be excited by an act of *courageous sacrifice. We can be excited by a beautiful day or by expectations of an upcoming holiday. We can also be excited by immoral things. Just consider the mainstays of successful Hollywood movies: gratuitous sex and violence. Although these may be exciting, they do not warrant our serious attention.

reason to be meaningful; what is
and emotions to be stimulating.

*"Be not hurried away
by excitement."*

Epictetus
*How the Semblances of Things
Are to Be Combatted, 18*

ASK YOURSELF:
*Is this thing something I experience
as stimulating? Might
others legitimately disagree with me? If so, it
is something exciting
rather than important.*

Individualism

The ideal of self-government

Individualism insists on the irreducible importance of each person. No person should be seen as just a piece of the larger social fabric, able to be sacrificed for the common good. *Respecting ourselves and others as individuals actually strengthens the *community, since it promotes real cooperation.

Individualism encourages *creativity. It stresses the importance of personal initiative and *responsibility. If I take the initiative, I am more likely to come up with new ideas and new ways of doing things. Also, if I help others because I want to rather than because I am forced to, I am more likely to succeed in supporting the community. Individualism encourages generous action.

Examples of individualism at work are plentiful in our culture. Democracy itself is an example of individualism: each *citizen has a right and a responsibility to be an active participant in government. Within the family, parents hope their children will grow in independence, developing their unique individual talents for their own *good and the good of those around them. By allowing each member of an organization or community to contribute individual gifts and by pooling these talents, the common good is served.

Individualism encourages self-motivated community; egoism encourages

ASK YOURSELF:
Does this ideal promote individual initiative? Does it encourage responsible action? If so, the ideal is individualism.

"A choice which intelligently manifests individuality enlarges the range of action and confers upon our desires greater insight and foresight, and makes choice more intelligent."

John Dewey
Philosophies of Freedom

Egoism

The ideal of selfishness

Egoism insists on the absolute priority of the individual. All relationships are entered into merely out of self-interest. Egoism is antithetical to all real *community. Treating others merely as means to personal satisfaction actually removes a key ingredient in individual *happiness — *friendship.

Egoism puts concern for ourselves first. It involves no sense of *responsibility. My own interest is always the bottom line. I consider my *creativity to be valuable only if it benefits me. If I help others, I do so merely because I believe such action will bring me what I want. Not only does my egoism weaken the community; it also denies me the experience of real cooperation and generosity.

Egoism is a danger, especially where individual initiative is encouraged. When the ultimate aim of the initiative turns from the *good of the individual within the context of community to the satisfaction of self-interest, egoism has replaced individualism. Democracy understood as the majority rule of merely selfish preferences is an obvious danger to *justice, for it is possible for the majority to be wrong. A business based purely on what satisfies each individual's wants does not benefit from the creative cooperation of meaningful work.

---

initiative for the good of self and self-interest for its own sake.

"The ego has always been a paradox — it is the point from which you see, but it also makes you blind."

Bill Russell
Second Wind (1979)

ASK YOURSELF:
Does this ideal promote individual initiative? Does it encourage selfish action? If so, the ideal is egoism, not individualism.

Joy
Delight in good

Joy involves thought as well as emotion. It is an appreciation or approval of something *good, along with a *feeling of excitement. Joy is the opposite of sadness. In both joy and sadness, *reason leads, and there is some rational explanation for the emotion.

Since joy involves thoughtful appreciation, it always has an objective component and a universal appeal. When I rejoice in something such as the birth of a child or an act of generosity, the object of my joy is something I believe others would and should rejoice in, too. I can explain to others the reason for my joy, and I can expect that, when they understand the source of my joy, they will know and share the same joy.

We rejoice in many different good things. We rejoice in the beauty of nature and the beauty of artistic creations. We rejoice in well-earned success — whether our own or that of our friends — for we understand the good things that success brings, as well as the *virtue and effort required to achieve them. We rejoice at weddings and births, for we recognize the obvious *goodness of intimate *friendship and new life. All these objects of joy are real goods that we understand, delight in, and hold to be universally valuable.

Both joy and exuberance involve a heightening
intellectual appreciation of some

ASK YOURSELF:
Is my feeling of
delight tied to a
recognition of
some real good?
Is it possible to share
this recognition with
others? If so, I am joyful.

"We do not speak of joy except when delight follows reason; and so we do not ascribe joy to irrational animals."

Thomas Aquinas
Summa Theologica, I-II, Q. 31, art. 3

Exuberance

Emotional high

Exuberance primarily involves feeling. It need not include any appreciation or approval of value. Exuberance is the opposite of depression. In both exuberance and depression, emotion leads, unguided by conscious *reason and *choice.

Since exuberance is a *feeling, it is basically subjective — a response to stimulation or imagination. When I feel elated, my exuberance may have a psychological or chemical explanation, but I am not conscious of any reason for it. Because my exuberance is not tied to my awareness of some objective value of universal appeal, it is not something that I think others would and should share.

Whereas joy is tied in with the recognition of something good, exuberance may be merely a physical or psychological reaction to something. Unconscious factors, such as environmental conditions or the introduction of natural or artificial chemicals into the bloodstream, may cause exuberance. Exuberance may even be due to things that are *morally bad. Pornography and gratuitous violence may be stimulating and produce an emotional high, but they are degrading. Unlike joy, exuberance is not tied to objects of universal value.

---

of emotion, but joy is always tied to an real good, while exuberance is not.

"An exuberant health without any judgment to guide it will never make either a happy or a useful man."

Abraham Tucker
The Light of Home Pursued (1852), Vol. 2

ASK YOURSELF:
Is my feeling of delight more excitement than appreciation of good? Is this excitement incommunicable? If so, it is exuberance rather than joy.

Judgment

Discrimination between ideas and actions

Judgment distinguishes between *truth and falsehood, *good and *evil. Only by carefully judging can we make progress toward *wisdom or *virtue. To refuse to judge is to refuse to care. If we do not care, we will not try. If we do not try, we will not find *happiness.

It is difficult to judge other people's ideas and actions *fairly. We want to *respect their *freedom to choose, and we do not want to impose our judgments on them. However, such noble sentiments can be mistaken. If I am wrong in my ideas or actions, you do me no favor by leaving me in the darkness of my *error. It is no better for me than for you to be ignorant of the difference between truth and falsehood or good and evil. We must care for each other. This means helping each other to know the truth and to be good.

Every day, we face challenges that call for judgment. We must judge what we see on the TV news to distinguish truth from falsity and good actions or policies from bad ones. We must judge accurately the actions of our peers so that, when they are going to do something wrong (such as cheat or steal or sexually abuse someone), we refuse to go along and we try to dissuade them as well. It is vital that we judge the ideas and integrity of our *leaders so that we elect only the best candidates.

Judgment distinguishes good ideas and actions among people, ignoring

ASK YOURSELF:
Am I concerned with the truth of ideas and the goodness of actions? Am I ignoring all favoritism? If so, I am involved in the valuable act of judging.

"Remember, when the judgment's weak, the prejudice is strong."

Kane O'Hara
Midas, Act I, sc. 4

Prejudice
Discrimination between people

Prejudice prejudges people according to irrelevant criteria: gender, race, *wealth, social status, culture, etc. This is clearly unfair to them, but also bad for us, for we act unwisely and unfairly. Only by overcoming prejudice can we find *happiness in *truth and *goodness.

It is difficult not to prejudge people who are different from us, for we are all limited to some extent by our experiences and cultural formation. However, prejudging people is obviously unfair and undermines *community. If I have *power and I am prejudiced, I prevent others from succeeding. Not only is it bad for others, but it is also bad for me. By prejudging others according to irrelevant criteria, I rule out learning from them and, more important, willingly embrace what is false, thus making myself less *wise and *virtuous.

Examples of the dangers of prejudice are plentiful. The ethnic cleansing we have witnessed in Bosnia, Somalia, and Kosovo are the results, among other things, of prejudice. Closer to home, every time we turn away from someone who differs from us in wealth or education or background, we are guilty of prejudice. Only when people's actions are wrong should we judge them, and even then we must be careful to focus our judgment on the wrongdoing and not on the wrongdoer.

from bad ones; prejudice arbitrarily discriminates
the task of careful judgment.

"The good neighbor looks beyond the external accidents and discerns those inner qualities that make all men human and, therefore, brothers."

Martin Luther King, Jr.
"Strength to Love" (1963)

ASK YOURSELF:
Am I more concerned with whom I am judging than with what I am judging? Am I swayed by favoritism? If so, I am prejudging, not judging fairly.

81

Justice

Absolute standard for right action

To be just is always to treat other people as they deserve to be treated. The basic principles of justice are universal; they are naturally known to all. This does not mean that we are automatically just, but only that we can, in principle, discover what we should do in order to be just. Justice does not depend on constitutions or on the will of those in *power.

Since justice is more basic than law, it can and should correct bad laws. The principles of justice cannot be changed, but laws can be. If we find that a law is unjust, we should change it. Unlike law, justice does not depend on the will of those in power. Although laws may be inconsistent, justice is not. It is as wrong to cheat others today as it was at any time in the past. It is as wrong to kill the innocent in Africa as it is in the United States.

We expect others to treat us justly, and we understand that we should treat them the same way. This means taking no more than our share of the cake and contributing equally to household chores. It means following legitimate laws. It really is unjust to violate our traffic laws even though those in Britain are different and equally acceptable. Sometimes, justice and law can conflict; even if legal, it would always be unjust to enslave someone.

Laws constrain people within a the universal foundation

ASK YOURSELF:
Is what I am doing fair? Would all reasonable people understand this to be fair? If so, my choice of action conforms with justice.

"There is a law above all statutes written on the heart, and by that law, unchangeable and eternal, no man can be or hold a slave."

Frederick Douglass
My Bondage and My Freedom

Law

A society's standard for right action

To be lawful is always to treat people in ways that do not violate the rules passed by a government. Laws may vary from *community to community; they are not naturally known but must be learned. They may be based on constitutions or on the will of those in *power — whether one person, a small *group of people, or the majority, as in a democracy.

Since laws are products of human will, which can be good or bad, not all laws are necessarily just. For example, in a democracy which operates according to majority rule, it is possible that a law allowing slavery could be passed. Since laws can be changed depending on the will of those in power, it is also possible for laws to be inconsistent with each other. Thus, slavery was permissible in this country at one time and now is forbidden.

Examples of laws made by human beings are plentiful. They vary in importance and in universality, some being found in virtually all communities. There are laws about driving automobiles. There are laws about buying and selling and about paying taxes. These may differ in different countries, and they may be changed. Some laws, such as those against stealing, rape, and murder, tend to be universal and are rarely, if ever, subject to change.

particular society, but justice is for all good laws.

"Asked what he gained from philosophy, Aristotle answered, 'To do without being commanded what others do from fear of the laws.' "

Diogenes Laertius
Lives and Opinions of Eminent Philosophers, "Aristotle," 11

ASK YOURSELF:
Is what I am doing permitted in this state or country? Is it possible that it might not be permitted elsewhere? If so, my choice of action conforms with the law.

Knowledge

Actually integrated meaning

Knowledge is more than information: it grasps the meaning contained in the information. For there to be knowledge, there must be consciousness — specifically, self-consciousness. To have knowledge is to be aware that we understand.

In addition to being conscious, knowledge is integrated. It is not an isolated bit; rather, it is the interrelation between bits. If I know something, I see a connection. After integrating bits of sense experience and memory, I know that moving shape to be my friend Joe. In the same way, I understand that the black marks on my computer screen are meaningful words that themselves refer to *reality.

The range of knowledge covers all aspects of meaning, from mathematics to art. When I know that 2+2=4, I grasp a connection between the elements (numbers) and a function (addition). When I know a pine tree, I grasp the distinction between this kind of thing and other things like it, as well as unlike it. When I know that, if there is smoke, there must be fire, I grasp a causal connection. I also know that, if I should not kill human beings and Betty is a human being, then I should not kill Betty. When I know that this symphony is beautiful, I grasp an integration of parts within a whole.

Although knowledge and information may contain
alive and integrated by intelligence, whereas

ASK YOURSELF:
Do I grasp the meaning of this data? Am I conscious of its being integrated with other meaningful data? If so, I have knowledge.

"Man only truly lives by knowing; otherwise he simply performs, copying the daily habits of others, but conceiving nothing of his creative possibilities as a man."

Alice Walker
In Search of Our Mothers' Gardens (1983)

Information

Potentially integrated meaning

Information is data that can be understood. In itself, it is not living meaning. It is, as it were, in storage, whether in the natural world, in computers, or in the brain. None of these is aware that it has information; none knows.

Information, in itself, is discrete. It is found in isolated bits that await connection by a knower. My eye picks up patterns of light and shade and color. My computer stores patterns of positive and negative charges. Nature is a wealth of information waiting to be known. But these bits of information require a living consciousness to discover their meaning.

We live in the age of information. The explosion of ways of storing and transferring information in the last fifty years is phenomenal. Computers store enormous quantities of it. The Internet stores and transfers the information of millions of computers. Although more complex than a computer, the brain also can be said to store and transfer information. Without the mind, however, it could not know that it has any information. The informational resources available to us today — mathematical, scientific, *moral, and aesthetic — are greater than ever, but without active knowers, they remain meaningless.

---

the same content, in knowledge the content is
information is merely stored content.

*"How vain is learning
unless intelligence go with it."*

Joannes Stobaeus
*Florilegium, quoted by Montaigne
in Essays, Bk. 1, ch. 24*

ASK YOURSELF:
*Is this data able
to be consciously
grasped? Does it re-
quire a knower to be
actually meaningful?
If so, it is information,
not knowledge.*

85

Leader

One who shows others the right way

A leader sees what ought to be done, organizes the *community to get it done, and sets a *moral standard for the community by practicing what she preaches. A leader is concerned primarily that all her actions be good for the community, not whether they will be popular. Thus, leadership is centered on a concern for others rather than for ourselves.

Leadership requires both vision and practical expertise. If I am to be a good leader, I must have a good plan for the community; I must also be intelligent and experienced enough to be able to bring it to fruition. I must be practical enough to know what can reasonably be accomplished, and I must be a good motivator of people in order to get the cooperation necessary for success.

The captain of a sports team who demands a lot but also inspires others by working hard himself shows leadership. The older child who helps guide her younger siblings by word and deed shows leadership. The class president who sets an agenda of academic *excellence and community service and who is able to communicate the importance of these to her classmates is a good leader. Leadership is exemplified by the government official who thoughtfully proposes and consistently applies *fair policies for all.

First and foremost, the good leader keeps
whereas the trendsetter

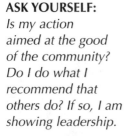

ASK YOURSELF:
*Is my action
aimed at the good
of the community?
Do I do what I
recommend that
others do? If so, I am
showing leadership.*

*"No ruler, insofar as he is a ruler, seeks
what is to his own advantage or orders it,
but that which is to the advantage of his
subject who is the concern of his craft;
this he keeps in view; all his words and
actions are directed to this end."*

Plato
The Republic, Bk. 1, 342e

Trendsetter

One who shows others a new way

A trendsetter sees what will be popular, convinces others to follow her, and sets a standard of fashion or action. A trendsetter is primarily concerned that people imitate her — not that she become more *virtuous. Thus, trendsetting is centered on concern for our own success and *popularity rather than for the well-being of others.

Although trendsetting need not involve any vision of what is really good for the *community, it does require intelligence and practical expertise. If I am to remain on the cutting edge, I must be able to read the crowd. I must be able to sense what the crowd wants and when what the crowd wants is changing. I must also be a good motivator if I am to get people to follow me.

Trendsetting occurs in many arenas, from clothes, to music, to ways of speaking and living, to *political action. The main focus in every case is to be popular. The fashionable dresser is a trendsetter. The student who runs for office on an agenda of fewer classes and more parties is a lifestyle trendsetter, not a leader. Developing a political strategy based on testing ideas by polls is reacting to popular opinion rather than leading by thoughtful example. A person who does so is seeking to be trendy rather than a good leader.

---

in mind what is best for the community,
is focused on being popular.

"Fads and fashions, the demands of popularity and success, enter where wisdom and experience should prevail."

Association of American Colleges
*Integrity in the College Curriculum,
New York Times, 11 February 1985*

ASK YOURSELF:
Is my action calculated to make others imitate me? Am I unconcerned for the good of the community? If so, I am courting popularity as a trendsetter, not showing leadership.

Love

The will to give of ourselves for another

Love is for the totality of another person. Some forms of love involve romantic and sensual feelings, but the essence of every love is thoughtful concern for another. Full human love flowers through *reason, affection, and free *choice. Love involves knowing and delighting in another, knowing what is *good, and willing that the other should have that good.

In love, giving is primary. At first glance, I might think that the important thing about love is that I am loved. But when I think about it, I realize that I love only if I give. Mutual giving and receiving is, of course, the ideal, but being in love is more about my doing good for another than about having something done for me. It is significant that we speak of "making" love, for love does not just happen. If it is to be real, we must make it real.

Love may exist on many levels: among family members, among friends, among neighbors, or among people of various cultures. A mother's love for her child is the paradigm case of love, since it is pure giving. The mother gives freely without expecting anything in return. The most perfect love involves such devotion on both sides. Such mutual selfless giving is rare. Still, it is the ideal for which *friendships, marriages, families, and *communities strive.

Love and lust both involve attraction, whereas lust is

ASK YOURSELF:
Do I care more for this person than for myself? Do I want what is best for this person? If so, my motivation is love.

"Love is a binding force by which another is joined to me and cherished as myself."

Thomas Aquinas
Summa Theologica, I, Q. 20, art. 1

Lust

The desire to take another for ourselves

Lust is for the gratification of ourselves. It is the desire to satisfy our sensual appetite by using another human being. Far from being centered in the distinctively human activities of *reason and free *choice, lust enslaves these. It cares nothing about knowing and delighting in another person, knowing what is *good, or willing that good for the other.

In lust, getting is primary. If I am moved by lust, my interest is in getting what I want — in this case, sexual satisfaction. I am inwardly directed. Even if the lust is mutually satisfied, it fails to involve the other at its center. In a case of a relationship based just on sex, each party is self-interested in the same way. Even our terminology points out this impersonal quality: we speak of "having" sex, as if it were something we owned.

Lust usually refers to selfish sexual desire, but it is possible to lust for money, *fame, or other things. Lust is a desire for things, or for people as things. More precisely, lust seeks its own satisfaction, and the objects of lust (whether things or people) are the means to that end. Thus, when we lust for a new car or when we lust after another person, we really desire satisfaction. Lust is radically selfish. It erodes the love that is the foundation of every *community.

---

but love is expressed in giving, expressed in taking.

"If he have not virtue, man is the most unholy and the most savage of all animals, and the most full of lust and gluttony."

Aristotle
Politics 1253a31

≈

ASK YOURSELF:
Am I interested in this person because of a desire for sexual pleasure? Am I unconcerned about this person's well-being? If so, my motivation is lust.

89

Maturity

Moral coming of age

To be mature is to have achieved *moral self-directedness and to have accepted *responsibility for our actions. A mature person is able and willing to take an active part in the *community.

Maturity is not necessarily a matter of age. It is not a stage of biological growth or legal status; rather, it must be freely chosen. Young people who are not biologically or legally considered adults are mature if their actions are guided by *reason and *virtue. Conversely, people who have reached the biological and legal age of adulthood are not necessarily mature. They may be guided by *impulse and *imagination rather than by reason. They may value things according to whether they bring *pleasure and *pain rather than according to whether they are *good or *evil, right or wrong.

Maturity is evident when we are ready to accept responsibility and *leadership. This happens in stages and at different times for different people. Even young children may show maturity by being willing to help their younger siblings or by settling their differences without fighting. High school students show maturity when they give of their time to help others or set good examples for their peers by their *leadership. Sacrificing self-interest for the sake of the other's good and the good of the family is a paradigm of maturity.

Maturity is the ability and willingness
adulthood is merely the arrival at

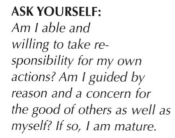

ASK YOURSELF:
Am I able and willing to take responsibility for my own actions? Am I guided by reason and a concern for the good of others as well as myself? If so, I am mature.

"It is not a sign of weakness, but a sign of high maturity, to rise to the level of self-criticism."

Martin Luther King, Jr.
Where Do We Go From Here? (1968)

Adulthood

Biological or legal coming of age

To be an adult is to have achieved full physical and mental growth or to have received full membership in a *community. It does not mean that one participates responsibly in the community.

Adulthood is basically a matter of age. It is a stage of biological growth or legal status, not a result of free will. At a certain point (which varies among cultures, depending on their legal and social rules, but corresponds roughly with biological maturity) a young person inherits full *rights and is therefore considered legally an adult. The fact of having inherited these rights, however, does not mean that the person is ready or willing to accept the *responsibilities that these rights imply. Such an acceptance is more a matter of *moral maturity than of physical and mental development.

Biologically, we attain adulthood when we are sexually mature and can reproduce. At about the same time, we achieve what is close to full strength and physical ability. Marks of adulthood in our society are age-oriented. At eighteen we attain legal status as full adults and can sign our own legal documents. We get the right to vote. At twenty-one we are allowed to consume alcohol. We must be twenty-five before we can rent a car. Moral maturity is not attained merely by arriving at any of these milestones.

---

to take on moral responsibility;
full biological or legal stature.

"A boy becomes an adult three years before his parents think he does, and about two years after he thinks he does."

Lewis B. Hershey
News Summaries, 31 December 1951

ASK YOURSELF:
Am I fully grown physically and mentally? Have I been accorded full legal status by society? If so, I am an adult, but not necessarily mature.

Mercy

Pardon for wrong done

Through *love for the wrongdoer and *hope for his renewal, mercy does not punish the wrongdoer as severely as he deserves. Mercy is possible only where there are *moral standards and the conviction that an act deserves *punishment.

There are good reasons for me to be merciful to you. Perhaps the circumstances of your action are unclear to me. In most cases I cannot be absolutely sure about your intentions — what you meant to do. Or perhaps you did wrong under enormous external pressure from peers or under the influence of a corrupt society. My mercy gives you the chance to do right. It manifests my belief that you can and want to do right and that my *forgiveness in this case will help you in your efforts to be good.

Mercy is for exceptional cases. It is merciful to forgive the *rudeness of a friend. Perhaps the friend was in a hurry or not feeling well. But it would not be merciful to ignore continuous rudeness. Mercy might not exact *fair punishment in a case where the punishment would ruin the wrongdoer's life. For example, mercy might not insist on expulsion from school for an infraction of the rules. Or mercy might not insist on punishment in a case where the punishment might be more than the wrongdoer can bear.

Mercy cares deeply for justice and laxness, on the other hand,

ASK YOURSELF:
Is this person's action wrong? Would my withholding punishment really be good for the person? If so, my withholding is an act of mercy.

"What is mercy but a fellow feeling for another's misery, which prompts us to help him if we can. And this emotion is obedient to reason, when mercy is shown without violating justice, as when the poor are relieved, or the penitent forgiven."

Augustine
City of God, Bk. 9, ch. 5

Laxness

Indifference to wrong done

Like mercy, laxness does not punish the wrongdoer as severely as he deserves. However, unlike mercy, *indifference rather than *love is the motive for laxness. Laxness exists when moral standards are low or nonexistent. It does not care whether an act deserves *punishment.

There are no good reasons for me to be lax. My laxness does not result from my awareness of special circumstances regarding your situation; rather, it is a general defect in my *moral attitude. I just do not care about you. Or perhaps I am motivated by self-interest: I do not punish you because I hope that I will not be punished when I do wrong. Unlike mercy, my laxness is not good for you, for my indifference gives you no support in your quest to understand and to do what is right.

Laxness does not restrict itself to exceptional cases; rather, it freely dispenses with standards of good behavior. Letting the bad behavior of children go completely unchecked is an example of laxness. Letting courtesy slide in schools so that students are not expected to treat each other or their teachers with respect is another example. Laxness is exemplified in the failure to enforce discipline on a sports team. Such laxness is bad for the individual players and for the team as a whole. Indifference helps no one.

---

for the good of the wrongdoer;
is indifferent to both.

"Blame [delinquency on] the moral carelessness that parents pass off as the gift of freedom as they cut their children loose like colorful kites and wish them an exciting flight."

Roger Rosenblatt
Time, 6 October 1986

ASK YOURSELF:
Am I indifferent to the morality of the person's action? Would my withholding punishment be bad for the person? If so, my withholding is an act of laxness.

Morality

What we should do

Morality is an ideal we should strive to follow, not an account of how we do, in fact, act. Morality is not universally practiced, but it ought to be. To be fully moral is to be good all the time.

Everyone has direct access to the basic principles of morality. I do not need to be taught them. All I need to do is reflect on what is *good and then never choose a lesser good over a greater good. For example, both food and human life are good, but because food is for the sake of life, it would always be wrong to choose food over life. Some things are good in themselves — life, *knowledge, and *friendship. I should promote these things for myself and for others and be sure that I do not violate them. Since these basic principles of morality are objective, they cannot be changed.

Morality is composed of universal imperatives. The strongest and most specific are negative. Do not kill. Do not rape. Do not lie. We understand these prohibitions simply by being human and reflecting on what that means. We know immediately that life, bodily integrity, and the desire to know the truth are good and should not be violated, whether the case concerns ourselves or others. There are also positive obligations. Help those who are in need. *Respect your elders. Develop your talents.

Customs are the habits of particular
of morality outline

ASK YOURSELF:
Is this action something I think that everyone should do or not do? Could I figure out its goodness or badness if nobody taught me? If so, it is a matter of morality, not just custom.

"The most important human endeavor is the striving for morality. Only morality can give beauty and dignity to life."

Albert Einstein
From a letter to a minister (1950)

Custom

What we do

Customs are the ways we do things, not ideals we are obliged to follow. Although customs may be universally practiced within a *group, they are not necessarily what ought to be done.

Because customs arise from specific cultural and social conditions, I do not have immediate access to all of them. I cannot discover customs simply by reflecting on what is *good in general. I learn them either directly from those who practice them or indirectly through some mode of communication (books, radio, television). To the extent that customs bind people together, they are good, for communal life is good. However, not all customs are good; if bad, they should be abandoned. Because customs are not objective, but based on the habits of people, they can be changed.

Customs reflect *community preferences. If customs involve imperatives, these imperatives presuppose acceptance of the standards of a culture or community. For example, in our culture it is customary to shake hands in greeting, but in Asia, this is not the custom (except as they have adopted Western customs). In our country, it is customary to celebrate July Fourth and Labor Day, but these customs are not observed in Europe. Neither culture is right or wrong, for customs are not universally obligatory.

communities, but the principles
duties for all.

"There is no more ridiculous opinion than to believe that all customs and laws of nations are inherently just."

Cicero
On Law, Bk. 1, ch. 15

ASK YOURSELF:
Is this action something I do but not something I think that everyone should do? Does my knowledge of its appropriateness depend on my culture? If so it is a matter of custom, not morality.

Mystery

Reality that transcends all knowledge

A mystery is something to be contemplated and lived. It is valuable in itself as a source of endless *wonder. Although a mystery transcends *knowledge, it is not meaningless. To meditate on a mystery is to enter ever-deepening realms of meaning.

A mystery is something that I see involves my very being. It is not something that I can stand outside of and objectify in order to put it to use for my benefit. A mystery in some sense stands above me and raises me up. It is not that I cannot understand a mystery at all, just that I cannot understand it completely. Mysteries are endlessly knowable.

There are, of course, religious mysteries, but there are also natural ones. The human being is a mystery. For we are at once body and mind — on the one hand bound by the laws of physics, on the other transcending them in thought and *freedom. *Love is a mystery to be lived, not a problem to be solved. To objectify love is to lose it. Then there is the radical mystery of existence itself. We cannot explain why there is anything at all, why there is not simply nothing. The proper intellectual response to mystery is wonder. Mysteries are neither to be solved nor put aside: they are truths open to endless contemplation.

A problem is a temporary challenge to a permanent challenge to knowledge

ASK YOURSELF:
Does this puzzling reality go beyond my knowledge? Is it beyond solution, but not a contradiction? If so, it is a mystery.

"A Mystery is an invitation to the mind. For it means that there is an inexhaustible well of Truth from which the mind may drink and drink again in the certainty that the well will never run dry, that there will always be water for the mind's thirst."

Frank Sheed
Theology and Sanity, Ch. 1

Problem

Reality that challenges our knowledge

A problem is something to be solved. In itself it has no value; its value lies in the solution it prompts. Although a problem transcends *knowledge, it does so in a limited way, and so its transcendence is temporary, lasting only until a solution is found.

A problem is something that I see needs to be objectified and then solved. It is something that prevents me from further knowledge or action. My purpose in solving it is to move on. Solving problems is useful to me. Although temporarily a setback, a problem does not stand above me. In overcoming a problem, I raise myself above it.

Problems present themselves to us every day. We are given math problems to solve in school. At first we do not know how they can be solved, but eventually we master them. We must figure out how to juggle our time to get all our errands done. This is an ongoing problem, but hardly a mystery. There are civic problems: How can we build a good interstate system at a reasonable cost to taxpayers? What is the best way to use our limited funds in building the new school? All these problems are objective problems to be solved, not transcendent mysteries to be lived. (Even a mystery story is really just a complex problem with a solution.)

---

knowledge to be overcome; a mystery is
and can only be lived in wonder.

"A question to be answered, an ambiguity
to be resolved, sets up an end and
holds the current of ideas to a
definite channel. The problem fixes
the end of thought and the end
controls the process of thinking."

John Dewey
How We Think, Pt. 1, ch. 1, sect. 3

ASK YOURSELF:
*Does this puzzling
reality go beyond
my knowledge?
Can I see in principle how it can
be solved? If so,
it is a problem.*

Norm

The way things ought to be

A norm is a standard of perfection for a certain kind of thing or behavior. It is implied in all evaluations. We can *judge things or behaviors to be more or less true or perfect only if there is something against which they can be measured.

A norm comes from within. It is a standard against which I compare things and by which I judge whether the things measure up or fail to measure up to what they should be. Thus, the norm for an eye is that it see with 20/20 vision. If my eyes fail to see this well, they are not normal. The norm for mature human beings is to be *wise and kind. To the extent that we are unwise or unkind, we fail to measure up to the norm for humanity.

We can talk about norms on many levels. Biologically, the norm for an apple tree is to be a healthy mature tree bearing plentiful fruit every year. The norm for a pen is to write clearly and easily with no blotting until all the ink is gone. Activities also have norms. The norm for driving an automobile is to obey all traffic *laws and to drive safely. *Moral norms are the ideals of human behavior: Be *honest; be *fair; do not kill; do not lie; help others. This is how human beings ought to act, even though it is a fact that we human beings fail to live up to these ideals.

A norm is a standard against which we
or actions; an average is a record of

ASK YOURSELF:
*Am I judging
the quality of a
thing or action?
Is my judgment based
on the knowledge
of what it should be? If
so, I am using a norm.*

*"Let us raise a standard
to which the wise and
honest can repair."*

George Washington
*During discussion,
Constitutional Convention (1787)*

Average

The way things tend to be

An average is what is typical of a certain kind of thing or behavior. It is derived from surveying the members of a group of things or activities. An average tells us nothing about the way the thing or behavior ought to be, only how it usually is.

An average comes from without. To find an average, I examine the members of some group of things or activities and come up with a factual description of the group. Thus, the average eyesight is less than 20/20: about half of the population needs glasses. Averages always refer to this or that particular sample of things, not to their nature or the way they should be. A statistical "norm" is not a norm at all, but only an average.

If we consider averages, we shall find variations depending on our sample group. The average apple tree in New Hampshire might be healthy 80 percent of the time and yield abundantly only 60 percent of the time. Worldwide, the averages might be somewhat lower. The average pen blots before the ink runs out. The average driver breaks the traffic *laws from time to time — by driving too fast or failing to signal properly. *Morally, we all fall short of obeying the ideals of *honesty, *justice, truthfulness, and kindness. Averages are behavioral descriptions, not norms.

---

measure the relative perfection of things
how things or actions usually are.

⬎

"If I could explain it to
the average person, I wouldn't
have been worth the Nobel Prize."

Richard P. Feynman
People, 22 July 1985

ASK YOURSELF:
*Am I describing the
usual quality of things or
actions? Is my description
based on observing and
recording many examples
of the thing or action? If
so, I am taking an average.*

Obedience

Free adherence to the will of a superior

Obedience comes from the Latin word *audire,* which means "to listen to." To be obedient is to hear, understand, and accept the guidance of another. Obedience is active: it is a *choice one makes to follow a worthy *authority.

Ideally, the authority I obey or follow should be wise and *virtuous. If this is so, my obedience to such an authority benefits both me and the *community. By listening to and following the advice of such a person, I can learn and begin to grow wise myself. The community is strengthened, for we choose to live in an orderly way. Even if it is not wise and *good, as long as the authority has been duly appointed, I should obey it for the good of the community.

True obedience is found only where the one who commands has the right to command and the one who obeys does so freely. Such obedience is exemplified in many of our relationships. Generally, the child should be obedient to the parent, the student to the teacher, and the athlete to the coach. This is not arbitrary. It is necessary for social order and is often of great benefit for the one who is obedient. The superior experience and *wisdom of the parent really can benefit the child. The teacher or coach, because of superior *knowledge, really can help the student or athlete.

Although obedience may look like servility,
choice, whereas servility implies the

ASK YOURSELF:
*Do I recognize
the legitimacy of
the authority and
the authority's rules?
Am I following the
authority freely? If
so, I am obedient.*

*"A slave cannot be obedient.
A thing which cannot
disobey is not obedient;
obedience is a choice."*

G. K. Chesterton
Chesterton Review 14, nos. 3-4: 217

Servility

Capitulation to the will of the powerful

Servility comes from the Latin word *servus,* which means "slave." To be servile is to follow another's direction because we have to, "or else." Thus, servility is passive: it is a reaction to the imposition of *power.

Servility is paid to another without regard to the legitimacy of that person's *authority or to that person's *wisdom and *goodness. For me to serve another blindly would be bad for both the *community and me. Even though blindly following such arbitrary orders may preserve my material well-being, it will prevent me from learning and from *maturing in wisdom. A society of servile people would lack the freely accepted order of a real community.

Servility is most clear in relationships in which the one who commands does not have the right to do so and the one who complies does so unwillingly. The relationship of the weak student to the school bully is servile. Also servile is a relationship in which the one who follows orders does so, not out of *respect for the one who orders or for that person's office, but out of some self-serving motive. The employee who follows what is clearly incompetent advice from a manager without comment, just to move up the ladder, is servile, not obedient.

---

obedience involves a free and intelligent abandonment of our will and intellect.

"A Briton even in love should be a subject, not a slave!"

William Wordsworth
Ere with Cold Beads of Midnight Dew

ASK YOURSELF:
Is the authority illegitimate or the authority's rules arbitrary? Am I doing what the authority says merely to avoid punishment or to get ahead? If so, I am servile.

101

Open-mindedness

Refusal to prejudge ideas

Open-mindedness gives each idea a *fair hearing. This implies fixed standards of *truth and *justice. Open-mindedness involves an active *choice to engage in the lives and ideas of others. It refuses to reject ideas without good reason. It is an attitude of welcoming, requiring effort and thoughtful consideration.

Such engagement is clearly good both for others and for ourselves. Obviously, my open-mindedness is good for you in the sense that it allows you to get a fair hearing for your ideas and an *equal opportunity to pursue what you see as *good. Open-mindedness is essential for building a fair and vibrant *community. But my open-mindedness is also good for me. It prevents me from making arbitrary *judgments about others, which would rule out the possibility of my learning from them.

Open-mindedness is good in most cases. We should be open to people of different races, nationalities, and *customs. We should be open to new ideas, whether scientific or *political. The limit of our duty to be open-minded comes when we are asked to believe that there is no truth or that no actions are right or wrong. To be open to these suggestions is to cease to think and to cease to care. To be open to the denial of everything without distinction is to be *indifferent.

Open-mindedness is fair judgment and indiscrimination, through refusing to

ASK YOURSELF:
Am I withholding judgment because of a real desire to know the truth? Do I care about what is best for others? If so, I am being open-minded.

"I shall adopt new views as fast as they shall appear to be true views."

Abraham Lincoln
Letter to Horace Greeley, 22 August 1862

Indiscrimination

Inability or refusal to judge ideas

In accepting all ideas, indiscrimination fails to give each idea a *fair hearing. It simply accepts everybody's ideas — true and false, *good and bad. With no fixed standards of *truth or *justice, it cannot be fair. It does not actively seek to understand and appreciate people and their ideas. It is a thoughtless and careless *indifference.

Such disengagement is clearly bad for others and for me. If I indiscriminately accept your ideas, I can hardly be said to care about you. Yes, I really ought to listen carefully to your ideas with an open mind, but if I understand some of your ideas to be false or *morally *evil and do not indicate this to you, I am being dishonest and uncaring about your well-being. This dishonesty and lack of care are clearly bad for me as well, since they corrupt my own search for what is true and good.

Indiscrimination is bad in most cases. The indiscriminate acceptance of all that we read in newspapers or see on TV is certainly not to be encouraged. We should not just accept all scientific and *political ideas; some of them may be false or involve immoral actions. The indiscriminate acceptance of the clothes people wear and the foods they eat matters little. But generally, indiscrimination is at odds with our *responsibility to make reasonable *judgments.

---

the path to learning and community;
judge at all, is the path to nowhere.

"Public opinion, in itself, has no criterion of discrimination, nor has it the ability to extract the substantive element it contains and raise it to precise knowledge."

G. W. F. Hegel
Philosophy of Right, Sect. 318

ASK YOURSELF:
Am I withholding judgment because I do not care or it is too much trouble to decide? Am I ignoring the well-being of others? If so, I am being indiscriminate, not open-minded.

Pain

Bad suffered

Pain is intimately tied up with our animal nature. It is something that we undergo rather than do. The prerequisite for experiencing pain is having a body with senses. Most of the pain we suffer is not due to our free *choices.

We see pain as bad because it hurts. In fact, we may think that the main purpose of life is to seek *pleasure and avoid pain. But such a position is wrongheaded. Pain is, in many respects, a good thing. For example, it keeps me from stepping into fires. It tells me when it is time to eat and drink. Without pain, I could not survive. Not all pain, of course, is good for me. There is pain that I need not suffer, such as the pain I feel because of accidents or when other people intentionally hurt me. However, such suffering does not make me *morally worse and may even be an occasion to gain the *virtues of *patience and *courage.

Although we can always avoid doing evil, we cannot always avoid suffering pain. Besides the pain that others inflict on us intentionally, there is a fair amount of pain that is not anyone's fault. We could be hurt by someone in a soccer match or when working on a construction project. We could be hit by a falling branch. These are bad for us physically, but do not make us morally worse.

As animals we naturally avoid pain; always to avoid the evil of doing

ASK YOURSELF:
*Am I feeling some-
thing that I do not
like? Is it some-
thing that I undergo
against my will?
If so, it is pain
and not evil.*

*"Pain is no evil,
Unless it conquer us."*

Charles Kingsley
St. Maura

Evil

Bad done

Evil is intimately tied up with our rational nature. It is something we do rather than undergo. The prerequisites for doing evil are *knowledge and free *choice. Only if we know something is wrong and choose to do it can we be said to do evil.

If you were asked whether you would rather suffer pain or do what is wrong, you might consider the answer obvious. After all, to do things that are wrong can be fun, and pain hurts. But such a conclusion is radically mistaken. I often excuse my evil actions (seeing them as *good) because they satisfy my natural desires. However, doing evil always hurts me at the very core of my being; it corrupts my *character. By doing what I know should not be done, I put myself in a kind of *moral contradiction, choosing evil as if it were good. This may or may not cause pain to others, but it always makes me morally worse.

It is possible to avoid doing evil. All immoral actions involve evil intentions. We lie to escape *punishment. We are *rude to others because it makes us feel superior. However, it is never the case that we must do these things. Nobody can force us to do evil. But whenever we do evil, we inevitably become worse human beings, for our actions form our character.

---

as rational animals we ought
what we know to be wrong.

"Doing what is unjust is more to be guarded against than suffering it."

Plato
Gorgias 527b

ASK YOURSELF:
Am I doing something that I know I ought not to do? Is it something that I willingly choose to do? If so, it is evil, not pain.

Patience

The willingness to wait for what is good

It is often the case that good things take time to develop. It is important to have the patience to wait for them. If we are impatient, we will miss out on many good things, or we may distort or ruin them by acting too quickly.

Patience is not sloth, for patience requires continuous *commitment, whereas sloth is a total lack of commitment. Sometimes the only way to get something good is to wait. If I am patient, I have *hope: I believe that the anticipated *good will come. But patience also requires *courage: I may have to persevere in patience for some time, not succumbing to the fear of failure.

Patience is necessary for any sustained personal or communal growth. Anything difficult in our lives requires patience. We need to be patient with ourselves when learning a language or learning to play an instrument. We need patience to endure suffering, whether physical or mental. We need to be patient with others when developing *friendships, for we all have our personality quirks that can sometimes be trying. Patience is required for establishing and nurturing common enterprises, from sports teams to governments. Wherever an activity requires another person's free cooperation, we must be patient.

Patience is not passivity, for patience
fruition in due time, while passivity

⌁

ASK YOURSELF:
Am I willing to wait for
something to develop? Is
this because I understand
that this kind of thing only
develops over time and
requires continuous commitment? If so, I am being patient.

*"A man's patience is that whereby
he bears evil with an even mind lest
he abandon with an uneven mind
the goods whereby he may
advance to better things."*

Augustine
On Patience, 2

106

Passivity

The unwillingness to act for what is good

Not all things come in due time. Sometimes we must act rather than wait. To be passive and leave everything up to fate is to fail to make good use of the intelligence and creative *freedom that have been granted us.

Passivity is close to sloth, for, like sloth, it does not care enough to make an effort. Also, like sloth, passivity is close to despair. Since I am *indifferent about the value of anything, I conclude that there is nothing worth doing, no ideal worth striving for. Passivity lacks hope and may also involve *cowardice: I refuse to strive for what is good through fear of failure.

Passivity prevents personal and communal growth. If we are to overcome difficulties in our lives, we must take action. Passivity is obviously disastrous for learning, since we can learn only if we make the effort to focus our intelligence on finding the truth. There are times when we must combat our suffering and not just accept it: we ought not to be masochistic or cease to care. Passivity undermines *community at all levels. *Friendships cannot thrive if friends do not give to each other. Common enterprises — from local organizations to state and national governments — will fail if their members are passive.

---

actively wills that some good come to
refuses to act for any good at all.

"I do not believe in a fate that falls on men however they act; but I do believe in a fate that falls on them unless they act."

G. K. Chesterton
Generally Speaking (1929), ch. 20

ASK YOURSELF:
Am I willing to wait for something to develop? Is this because I am not willing to make the effort or commitment necessary to bring it about? If so, I am being passive, not patient.

Patriotism

Appropriate devotion to country

Patriotism is based on an accurate appraisal of our country and our relationship to it. Patriotism is not a blind love of country. It involves an appreciation for what our country has done for us, but also an evaluation of the *justice of its policies.

There is room for a certain degree of loyalty to my country simply because it is my own, just as I should be loyal to my family, school, and town. But I must balance this with the realization that other people have the same loyalty to their country, family, school, and town. Since we all have received benefits from these institutions, we really do have an obligation to *respect, protect, and nurture them. But this obligation should not blind us to defects in our institutions and our awareness of our obligation to correct them.

The Romans thought that the most noble thing that we could do would be to die for our country. In the twentieth century, it is clear that patriotism helped defeat unjust aggression. Unless some people had been willing to fight for family, *community, and country, the world would be a very different place today. Still, it is essential that patriotism be linked to a just cause. True love of country means devotion to its *moral improvement as well as to its preservation.

Patriotism is appropriate loyalty to one's support for one's country even

"Patriotism is when love of your own people comes first; nationalism, when hate for people other than your own comes first."

Charles de Gaulle
Life, 9 May 1969

Nationalism

Irrational devotion to country

Nationalism goes beyond an accurate appraisal of our country and our relationship to it. It is a blind love of country. It may involve appreciating the *good our country has done for us, but it does not include an evaluation of the *justice of its policies.

In nationalism my loyalty to my country is overplayed, and I fail to keep in mind that other people have similar loyalties to their countries. To be loyal to my country is good, but it is arbitrary and indefensible to think that, just because it is my own, my country really is in truth better than all other countries. Nationalism ignores the obligation to evaluate carefully the defects of our country and to work tirelessly to correct them. Instead of working to make my country better, nationalism declares it to be the best.

The twentieth century was filled with examples of the dangers of nationalism. First and foremost is the example of Hitler and Nazi Germany. Rampant German nationalism led to the atrocities of the holocaust and the attempt to subject Europe to German rule. Another example is the extreme nationalism of the Japanese, which prompted their attempt to dominate the East. More recently, Saddam Hussein in Iraq has encouraged nationalism as a way of fortifying his *power.

---

country; nationalism is fanatical
when the country is wrong.

" 'My country, right or wrong,' is a thing
that no patriot would think of saying
except in a desperate case. It is like
saying, 'My mother, drunk or sober.' "

G. K. Chesterton
The Defendant, 125

ASK YOURSELF:
*Do I love my
country because it is
mine? Am I uncon-
cerned about my
country's defects?
If so, my devotion
is nationalism.*

Peace

Presence of harmonious agreement

Peace is not just the absence of fighting: it is also the free integration and cooperation of a people. Peace includes both external harmony with others outside our *community and internal harmony among the members of the community.

For us to be at peace, it is necessary that we agree to live in accordance with a certain order. Peace is not simply an external process, such as putting blocks in order; if we wish to be at peace, we must cooperate with each other in establishing harmonious relationships. Thus, peace cannot be forced upon us by an external force, but must be based on a *free agreement of the people who make up a community. Since this order is based on free agreement, it tends to last.

Peace in a family involves each member's acting in a way that is conducive to the good of every other member. The same is generally true for peace in larger communities. Peace in a town or state requires the general agreement and cooperation of the *citizens on important things such as education and public services. The same holds true, but on a larger scale, for peace within a nation. The ideal of world peace involves a *commitment by all people to live in harmonious order.

A truce is an agreement to ignore integration of people who

ASK YOURSELF:
*Am I concerned
to establish harmony
with others? Is it essential that this harmony
be freely embraced
by them? If so, I am
seeking peace.*

*"Domestic peace is the well-ordered
concord between those in the family
that rule and those that obey. Civil peace
is a similar concord among the citizens.
Peace is the tranquillity of order."*

Augustine
City of God, Bk. 19, ch. 13

Truce

Absence of strife

A truce is simply a state of affairs in which there is no fighting. It is mostly an external arrangement to live and let live. As such, a truce is a good thing; but it is a minimal good, lacking the rich harmonious relations of peace.

A truce does not require that we agree to live in accordance with a certain order, only that we agree not to fight each other. We may agree to a truce only reluctantly, under pressure from an external *power or because we are afraid. We may accept the truce, not because we agree with the other side, but merely because we fear the consequences if we do not accept it. Because it is not based on harmonious agreement, a truce is fragile and less likely than peace to last.

A truce among family members may be far from genuine peace. They do not fight with each other, but neither do they make the effort to establish mutually supportive relations. A truce between *political factions rejects open aggression, but it does not embrace any real cooperation. Most treaties between nations have more the character of truces than real peace. Their purpose is to prevent violence between the parties in question, rather than to nurture harmony among them.

---

differences, but peace is grounded in the share a vision of the common good.

"If one man be at concord with another because he is coerced by the fear of penalty and not of his own free will, then his condition is not one of peace."

Thomas Aquinas
Summa Theologica, II-II, Q. 29, art. 1

ASK YOURSELF:
Am I concerned to prevent open hostilities with others? Might this prevention be externally imposed on them if need be? If so, I am seeking a truce.

Politeness

Treating others with respect

Politeness is the genuine effort to treat others with courtesy and *respect — even those we do not know or may not like. Politeness is good for the *community. The selflessness of politeness sets a tone and standard of mutual goodwill.

Although being polite does not mean than I am *virtuous, the effort required to be courteous can lead me in the right direction. There are many instances in life where I learn by doing — learning to walk and talk, to play a musical instrument, to become a competent surgeon. It is the same with *moral matters: I become virtuous by doing virtuous actions. Although courteous action may not imply respect on the deepest conscious level, development of polite habits paves the way for deeper *virtue and selfless action.

Politeness is marked by a genuine desire to put others at ease. Opportunities to do so are plentiful. We might begin by making the consistent effort to say *please* and *thank you* when dealing with those around us. We could show our respect for the elderly by letting them go first or by giving up our seats for them on a crowded bus or subway. We could engage a person who is being ignored in conversation and listen carefully to what he has to say, even if we are not particularly interested.

The truly polite person is gracious
the phony person is gracious

ASK YOURSELF:
*Do I treat all
whom I meet
with personal
attention? Do I
do so out of respect
for them? If so,
I am being polite.*

*"Politeness is artificial good humor;
it covers the natural want of it, and it
ends by rendering habitual a substitute
nearly equivalent to the real virtue."*

Thomas Jefferson
Writings, Vol. 12

Phoniness

Pretending to respect others

Phoniness is a fake show of *respect for others in order to protect or benefit ourselves. Such "courtesy" is all on the surface. It is not really commendable at all, since the key to all good actions is intention, and the intention here is selfish.

Although phoniness does not make me deeply immoral, pretense in my relations with others can prevent me from developing the *virtues of *honesty and *friendship. If I only pretend to be courteous to others, not only do I show disrespect for them, but I also end up developing habits of deception. If I become used to treating people with feigned consideration, I will find it difficult, if not impossible, to practice the real virtues of friendship and *love, much to my real loss. My phoniness paves the way for selfish isolation.

Phoniness can often be recognized by tone of voice. Courteous words may be there, but the tone is ironic. Sometimes we show phoniness by going way beyond what is appropriate in our signs of courtesy. We may make much of a person in order to show our superiority. Sometimes our polite communication is hurried, or we are distracted and clearly not interested in the other. All these signs of pretended courtesy in our relations with others may indicate a deeper disrespect beneath.

---

to others out of respect for them;
because it serves his purpose.

"Dissembling courtesy!
How fine this tyrant
Can tickle where
she wounds!"

William Shakespeare
Cymbeline, Act 1, sc. 1, l. 84

ASK YOURSELF:
Do I treat all
whom I meet with
personal attention?
Do I do so for my
sake more than
theirs? If so, I am
being phony.

Politics

The art of guiding a people well

Although we do not often see it today, politics, in its root meaning, is concern for the life of the *community. *Polis* is the Greek word for "city." Thus, to pursue politics is to pursue public service in the area of government. This is a noble activity.

Politics involves both an ideal vision of what communal life should be and the practical ability to bring about a community as close to that ideal as possible. If I am a politician in the traditional sense, I always keep the ideal of the common *good in mind. This — rather than party spirit — is my guiding light. If I am a good politician, I am also an expert in the practical art of making the ideal a reality. In this, politics is much like *prudence. But pragmatism in politics must always serve the ideal of a *virtuous and cooperative community.

Politics comes into play wherever there are communities that are self-governed. There is a need for vision and for consensus-building at the local, state, and national levels. At the local level, the nobility of political involvement is most obvious, for it is easier to make a real difference in a small community. Although partisanship increases as the political sphere widens, we should recognize and commend politicians who devote their lives to the public good.

Whereas partisanship aims at defending politics is guided by the ideal of a

ASK YOURSELF:
Am I concerned with the good of the community? Is my concern guided by a commitment to the well-being of the entire community? If so, I am practicing the venerable art of politics.

"Politics ought to be the part-time profession of every citizen who would protect the rights and privileges of free people and who would preserve what is good and fruitful in our national heritage."

Dwight D. Eisenhower
Address, 28 January 1954

114

Partisanship

The art of gaining and controlling power

Often, politics as we know it today is simply partisanship. Partisans do whatever they can to ensure that their party rules. Partisanship is interested in benefiting only part of the *community: the part with which the partisan identifies. Such activity is narrow and selfish.

Partisanship takes as its ideal the promotion of a party and works to bring about its ascendancy. There may be good reasons for my original allegiance to a *group; but once I become a partisan, I no longer question my group's goals and programs. Victory for my side replaces the ideal of the best community for all. I focus on the practical art of finding ways to achieve the goals of my faction and to institute its programs. My pragmatism serves and is guided by the faction — not by the ideal of a *virtuous and cooperative community.

Partisanship is most obvious in politics at the national level. Candidates spend an inordinate amount of time and energy showing why their faction should be in *power. This may be done by making policy statements about their plans or by attacking the policies of the opposing party. Personal attacks are also popular. Although such tactics are less obvious in the government of a local community, they still occur, much to the detriment of the public *good.

---

and promoting the wishes of a faction,
virtuous, harmonious community.

"The partisan, when he is engaged in a dispute, cares nothing about the rights of the question, but is anxious only to convince his hearers of his own assertions."

Socrates
Phaedo 85

ASK YOURSELF:
Am I concerned with the good of my party or faction? Is my concern indifferent to the well-being of the entire community? If so, I am practicing partisanship, not politics.

Profundity

Depth of meaning

What is profound may be hard to understand because it is complicated or mysterious. Even when presented clearly, what is profound has layers of meaning deeper than we can grasp. What is profound promises further insight: there is more to be understood than what the surface reveals.

Profundity is clearly a good thing, for it encourages me to think harder and to seek more complete understanding. Although I experience a certain tension in not understanding what is profound, it is the creative tension of *wonder, not the frustration of confusion. I do understand some of it from the very beginning, but I know that there is much more to be understood. The thinking needed to grasp what is profound is admittedly difficult, but the rewards are immediate as a world of deeper meaning opens up to me.

On a simple physical level, we might say that the experience of gazing into a star-filled sky is profound: there is more reality there than we, with our naked eye, can see. The universe, the nature of human thought, *freedom of *choice: these are profound *mysteries of *reality. In addition, there are profound books, poems, and works of art. They enrich us with insights into reality, the human condition, and beauty that go beyond our everyday lives.

Although both profundity and obscurity are hard to
its depth of meaning, obscurity

ASK YOURSELF:
Am I unable to
understand something? Is this because
the thing itself is
complex, rich, and
difficult? If so, I am
faced with profundity.

*"Truth, sir, is a profound sea,
and few there be who dare wade deep
enough to find out the bottom on't."*

George Farquhar
The Beaux' Stratagem, Act 5, sc. 1

Obscurity

Unclarity of thought or expression

What is obscure may be hard to understand because it is unclear or confused. Try as we may, we cannot see whether what is obscure has depths of meaning, for it is either poorly expressed or the thought itself is not coherent. Unlike profundity, obscurity holds out no promise of deeper understanding.

Obscurity is clearly not a good thing, for it prevents me from *knowing. My initial frustration and confusion when faced with obscurity do not yield to a more complete understanding. No matter how hard I think about what is obscure because of incoherence, I will not be able to understand it for the simple reason that there is nothing there to understand. If something is obscure, I have no inkling about its meaning, and there can be no growth in my understanding. Whatever hard thinking I may do must fail to bear fruit.

On a simple physical level, the experience of trying to look into a star-filled sky through thick fog is obscure: we cannot tell whether there are depths beyond us. Books, poems, and works of art may be obscure by accident, due to the incompetence of the writer or artist. Sometimes they are obscure by design, attempting thereby to imitate profundity. Such intentional obscurity shows a certain dishonesty and inspires confusion and fruitless labor in the audience.

---

understand, profundity is not understood because of because of its lack of meaning.

"Obscurity is the realm of error."

Vauvenargues
Réflexions et Maximes, No. 5

ASK YOURSELF:
Am I unable to understand something? Is this because the presentation of the thing is confused or its nature is incoherent? If so, I am faced with obscurity.

Progress

Becoming better

Most simply, progress implies movement in some kind of consistent direction. We can be said to be further along (to have progressed) only if we have been and continue to be going in the same direction.

Along with consistent direction, progress generally implies some improvement. Improvement, in turn, implies a standard that is not itself changing. Unless I have access to a fixed standard, I cannot tell whether things are getting better or worse. I must have an idea of what would count as ideal (e.g., mastery of nature for technology, complete knowledge of the universe for science) in order to recognize progress.

It is clear that the sciences and technology have progressed in the last three hundred years. This progress seems to keep step with the march of time. Year by year we gain a more precise understanding of the nature of our material world, and we develop better machines to get things done. The criteria of *simplicity and comprehensiveness provide standards of measurement in science. *Usefulness is our measure of progress in technology. By these standards, we can see that progress has clearly been made in these areas.

Progress and change differ mostly
cumulative advance over

⌇

ASK YOURSELF:
*Does this series
of events have
a consistent
direction? Does
it show improve-
ment? If so, it
is progress.*

*"The mechanical arts are continually
thriving and growing, at the first rude,
then convenient, afterwards adorned,
and at all times advancing."*

Francis Bacon
The New Organon, 74

Change

Becoming different

Change does not necessarily imply movement in any consistent direction. There need not be any continual advance. Change can go forward (progress) or backward (regress), or just lead to something different.

Although some criterion must be used to know that there is change, it need not be a standard measure. I can use any measure I please, and the measure can be changed as often as I please. It does not even matter if my standard itself is changing so long as it is not changing as fast as what I am measuring. Thus, I cannot really say that change, of itself, is for the better. It is just different. Novelty does not mean improvement.

The seemingly inevitable progress we see in the sciences and technology is not so evident in ethical behavior and artistic creation. These indeed have changed, but they do not seem to be getting better automatically with time. It is not clear that contemporary art is better than the art of the Renaissance. And Hitler certainly did not represent an advance in moral *leadership. Although it is certainly possible to have progress in art and *morality, it is not clear that we become more artistic and more ethical with each passing year.

in this: that progress implies a time, and change does not.

"It is the darling delusion of mankind that the world is progressive in religion, toleration, freedom, as it is progressive in machinery."

Moncure D. Conway
Dogma and Science

ASK YOURSELF:
Does this series of events lack a consistent direction? Is it unclear whether there is improvement? If so, it is change, not progress.

Proof

Conviction through evidence

Proof focuses on facts and on making connections between facts. Proof depends on objective evidence that is accessible to all. If the evidence is ordered in the proper way, everyone should agree with the proof's conclusion.

Proof proceeds according to the logic of agreement. If you and I agree that some statements of facts are true and I correctly point out a conclusion that follows from them, you should agree with my conclusion. I do not try to convince you against your better *judgment, but according to your best judgment. I appeal to *reason as an objective arbiter that stands above you and me. It is reason that shows me that I am right and reason that should get you to agree with me, whether or not you feel like it.

Proofs have many forms. They can be mathematical. If the sum of the angles of every triangle is 180 degrees, then the sum of the angles of an isosceles triangle is 180 degrees. Proofs can also be scientific. The hypothesis that water is heavier than gasoline can be proven to be true by pouring the two liquids into a container: the gasoline rises to the top. We can also have *moral proofs. Since all people should be treated with dignity, enslaving another human being is always wrong.

Both proof and persuasion aim at convincing while persuasion manipulates

ASK YOURSELF:
Do I understand the evidence presented? Do I see why the conclusion is inevitable? If so, I am assenting to proof.

"The proofs and demonstrations of logic are toward all men indifferent and the same."

Francis Bacon
The Advancement of Learning,
Bk. 2, ch. 18, sect. 5

Persuasion

Conviction through emotion

Persuasion focuses on appearances and on manipulating the *feelings and the *imagination of the audience. Persuasion depends on understanding and manipulating the subjective state of the hearer rather than proving objective *truth.

Persuasion proceeds according to the psychology of agreement. It does not so much matter that you and I agree on the facts or that I present them to you in an orderly way; what matters is that I get you to agree with me. This may mean that I get you to go against your better *judgment. I do not appeal to *reason as an objective arbiter; I use reason only if it will help me persuade you. I want you to feel that I am right, and if appealing illegitimately to your imagination and emotions helps me succeed, that is what I will do.

Persuasion comes into play wherever agreement is sought by means other than an appeal to objective evidence. It is not likely to be very successful in mathematics and science, since their methods rely heavily on logical proof and empirical facts. Persuasion is more likely to be used and to be successful where our purpose is to get others to do something. Advertisers, journalists, and politicians often try to persuade their audiences by appealing to various emotions and half-truths.

others, but proof appeals to facts and logic impressions and emotions.

"The art of persuasion consists as much in knowing how to please as in knowing how to convince, so much more do men follow caprice than reason."

Pascal
Geometrical Demonstration

ASK YOURSELF:
Does what is said appeal to my emotions or prejudices? Do I feel that the conclusion is right? If so, I am yielding to persuasion.

Prosperity

State of well-being

Prosperity is being well-off in this world, materially and spiritually. To prosper is to have in an orderly and vital balance the good aspects of life: material possessions, security, health, *knowledge, *friends, family, work, *virtue.

Prosperity is desired for its own sake and is therefore more ultimate than wealth, which is desired for the sake of what it can buy. Although prosperity concerns every aspect of my well-being, it has more to do with what I do and the kind of person I am than with what I have. This is because my actions and my state of *character are more central to my well-being than my possessions are. They are mine in the deeper sense, because they depend on my free *choices for their existence.

Prosperity is more than wealth and the things wealth can bring. Prosperity requires effort and includes things that cannot be bought: health, which calls for proper diet and exercise; meaningful participation in a vocation, which results from thoughtful choice and hard work; friends and family, which must be cultivated with *wisdom and sensitivity; education, which takes a continuous effort to know, not just schooling; virtue, which is the continuous effort to be good; appreciation of art; and giving of ourselves to the *community.

Although prosperity includes some wealth, it centers on knowing, creating, and loving

ASK YOURSELF:
Do I have adequate material means? Do I also participate in goods that cannot be bought, such as knowledge, friendship, and virtue? If so, I am prosperous.

"Who may be termed most prosperous? He who barters the perishable for the everlasting."

Solomon Ibn Gabirol
Mibhar ha-Peninim
(Choice of Pearls; c. 1050), No. 529

Wealth

Material possessions

Wealth is the means to material well-being in the world. To be wealthy is to be able to purchase things that money can buy. Wealth can provide us with security, *pleasure, health care, education, and a certain degree of *political *power.

Wealth is desired as a means to the things it can buy and is therefore less desirable than those things themselves. Thus, medical care and education are more important than the money to buy them. But they, too, are only means: health itself and *knowledge are more important still, and they cannot be guaranteed by medical care and an expensive education. Nor can wealth guarantee that I will have meaningful work or be *virtuous. These key aspects of prosperity cannot be bought.

Wealth is, of course, helpful in our lives. It enables us to provide essential items such as food, shelter, and medical care for ourselves and our families. But wealth also tends to distance us from other goods. If we focus all our attention on being wealthy, we spend less time cultivating *friends and family, pursuing *wisdom, and appreciating beauty. We may spend more time at recreation than at creating a meaningful world of *justice, and compassion — all of which require activity rather than purchasing power.

---

more on what we do than on what we have — more than on having material things.

"Nothing is so revealing of narrowness and littleness of soul than love for money."

Cicero
On Moral Obligation, Bk. 1, ch. 20

ASK YOURSELF:
Do I have the material means to purchase security, comfort, and power? Are these means sufficient for a lifetime? If so, I am wealthy.

Prudence

Reasonable caution in the face of difficulties

Prudence is the ability to apply *moral principles successfully to particular situations. Its aim is to bring about as much concrete good in the world as is possible. Because this may sometimes mean settling for less than perfection, prudence may seem overly cautious. Real prudence, however, avoids the waste of foolhardiness and wisely chooses the most *good presently possible.

Prudence requires experience. I must learn to *judge what is possible as well as what is good. The ideal is to bring as much good to the world as I can. But I cannot single-handedly solve all the world's problems. If I try to do what is impossible, I will fail. In some cases, compromise brings about the greatest good. Prudence is the ability to know when such compromise is appropriate.

In general, we know that we should help others. Prudence enables us to see how to be successful in helping others in particular cases. It is usually prudent to invest our resources so that we may help the needy in a regular way rather than giving all our money away at once. This will likely bring more good to others. It is prudent, not cowardly, to run away from a gang of thugs. It is prudent, not cowardly, for a nation not to engage in a war that it knows it cannot win.

Prudence exercises good judgment in difficult
good; cowardice deals with

ASK YOURSELF:
*Am I concerned
to bring about as
much good as possible?
Is this the best way to
do so in this situation?
If so, I am acting
prudently.*

"By prudence we understand the practical knowledge of things to be sought, and of things to be avoided."

Cicero
On Moral Virtues, Bk. 1, ch. 43

Cowardice

Disgraceful flight in the face of difficulties

Cowardice is the unwillingness to stand up to painful situations. It aims at preserving our own safety at any cost. Whereas prudence *wisely avoids a confrontation it cannot possibly win, cowardice refuses to confront any danger. In the face of adversity, the coward runs away. Unlike prudence, cowardice is not concerned with trying to bring about the most *good presently possible.

Cowardice is a kind of habit based on experience. If I am a coward, I turn and run from *pain and fear, and the more I do this, the more it becomes a matter of habit. As a coward, I abandon the difficult work of deciding when I should stand up for the good in the face of pain or possible failure and when I should compromise. I turn away from all difficult, painful, and dangerous situations.

In general, we desire to please ourselves and avoid what is painful. Cowardice is a constant option. It is often cowardice that prevents us from speaking up for *justice or defending the innocent when such positions are unpopular. We fear being ostracized by our peers. It is cowardice that keeps us from going to the aid of someone in trouble, even when we are the person's only hope and when we clearly have a good chance of saving the person without serious loss to ourselves.

situations, preserving and promoting concrete difficulty by running away.

"To know what is right and not do it is the worst cowardice."

Confucius
Analects, Bk. 2, ch. 24

ASK YOURSELF:
Am I concerned with my personal safety? Am I running away from a defense of the good because I am afraid? If so, I am a coward.

Punishment

Answering harm with penalty to satisfy justice

Proper punishment aims at the well-being of all members of the *community: the wronged, the wrongdoer, and society. Punishment should be deserved, and it should restore the community.

Although we tend to think of punishment as something to be avoided at all costs by the wrongdoer and pursued to the greatest degree possible by the offended party, neither position is reasonable. If I do wrong, I should be punished. If uncorrected, I am likely to grow *morally worse and so lose the possibility of finding *happiness. Equally, if I am wronged, I should desire only that justice be done. To desire punishment greater than what is deserved is to will *evil, which I should never do.

Consider what would be *fair punishment. As late as the seventeenth century in England, the punishment for stealing was death. Although death may be a plausible punishment for murder, it is clear that it is unsuitable for petty theft. Such a punishment, being unjust, must be bad for the society that imposes it, and it cannot be good for the thief. More appropriate might be incarceration, payment of a fine, and community service. Such punishments would help re-establish order in the community, restore what was taken, and punish the thief in a constructive way.

Punishment intends the good of justice and intends the evil of hurting another

ASK YOURSELF:
Is my judgment guided by a concern for the common good? Do I care for all involved, both the wronged and the wrongdoer? If so, my intention is to bring about fair punishment.

"Punishment makes sense only if, while affirming the needs of justice and discouraging crime, it serves man's renewal."

Pope John Paul II
Homily at Mass at Regina Coeli, Rome's oldest jail, 10 July 2000

Revenge

Answering harm with harm to gratify hatred

Revenge seeks to repay *evil with evil to satisfy personal animosity. It brings disorder to the *community by awakening anger and hatred in the one who is repaid.

We may feel like taking revenge when we have been wronged, but such a feeling should not be indulged. For although revenge is a response to an injury, it is not limited by what would be objectively best for all involved. Rather, I am ruled by subjective criteria: what I want and feel. Such feelings are understandable; but if I allow my feelings to govern instead of *reason, then what is to prevent me from punishing more than is *fair, or even punishing the innocent?

A sign of revenge is that it usually goes beyond what is fair: "If he insults me, I will beat him to a pulp!" Beating someone up is not a fair response to an insult; but because of the personal affront, my action feels justified. Revenge is often motivated by an inflated image of our own worth. A teacher who fails a student just because she asks tough questions is taking revenge. Gangs embrace a revenge mentality: "We will kill four of them for every one of us they kill." Revenge is motivated by a desire to harm the one who caused the injury, whether intentionally or not.

---

the restoration of the social order; revenge
and the gratification of hatred.

*"Revenge is a kind of wild justice;
which the more man's nature
runs to, the more ought law
to weed it out."*

Francis Bacon
Of Revenge

ASK YOURSELF:
*Is my judgment based
on an emotional hatred
for the person who has
done wrong? Do I wish
evil for this person? If so,
my intention is revenge,
not punishment.*

Questioning

The search for answers

Questioning challenges some *authority, whether it be our senses, someone else's statement, or even our own former *opinion. The purpose of questioning is to come to an answer. Questioning is essential for any intellectual or *moral growth. Without questions, we simply could not learn.

Every time we encounter something new, we have questions. When I have a question about *reality, I wonder what the answer could be, and I hope to find out. I place myself in the service of *truth. There is an implicit trust here — a trusting that reality is intelligible and that I can find out about it. Similarly, when I have a question about what I should do, I believe that I can find an answer.

There are all kinds of questions. How many square inches are there in a square yard? How far is it from Baltimore to Chicago? Is there a God? How can I live a better life? Which plan for the new school would provide a more pleasing environment in which to study? How can I get more power in my soccer kick? Questions invite answers. Whether our concern be the physical world, human nature, moral obligation, or beauty, questions draw us forward. They are our pathways into every realm of meaning.

Although questioning and skepticism both and the second to undermine,

ASK YOURSELF:
Do I believe that there is truth to be known? Do I challenge what I hear for the sake of attaining the truth? If so, I embrace the path of questioning.

"The important thing is not to stop questioning."

Albert Einstein

Skepticism

The rejection of all answers

Skepticism challenges all authorities, even the *authority of *reason. It denies that there are any answers to the questions we ask about *reality. If we doubt everything, intellectual and *moral growth is impossible. With skepticism, we simply cannot learn, and we cannot do good.

Unlike questioning, skepticism is not fed by *wonder but is choked by despair. If I am a skeptic, I give up on reality: I claim that there is no such thing as *truth. If I am a skeptic, I give up on doing good: I claim that no way of acting is better than any other. If skepticism is embraced, then questioning of any kind makes no sense; for if there are no answers, then there is no sense in seeking them.

Skepticism takes many forms. Limited skepticism is a close cousin of questioning. It challenges us to look at things in different ways. But skepticism as a general mental stance makes no sense. Skepticism is often introduced as a challenge to the certainty of our *knowledge of reality, our knowledge of ethical norms, and our knowledge of God. One way people seek to refute rational *argument is to argue that reason does not work. This is skepticism. Of course, if this is true, then the refutation does not work either.

---

challenge authority, the first does so to find,
what is true and good.

"I suppose it is true that a man can be a fundamental skeptic, but he cannot be anything else; certainly not even a defender of fundamental skepticism."

G. K. Chesterton
Saint Thomas Aquinas

ASK YOURSELF:
Do I deny that any truth can be known? Do I challenge what I hear for the sake of refuting all claims to truth? If so, I block the path of questioning and embrace skepticism.

129

Reality

All that is

Reality includes the material universe experienced by our senses and studied by science, but also such things as thought, free will, *moral principles, and *love. If these things are not real, then human life is meaningless.

If I restrict what is real to material things, thereby denying the immaterial reality of thought and ideas, I must also deny the reality of science. After all, the scientific method itself is a concept, not a material thing that can be perceived by the senses. Likewise, if I do not allow for the reality of free will, then even my choice to make science the definitive measure is not real. In short, ideas and *freedom of *choice transcend materiality.

*Justice, love, and freedom of choice are examples of realities that are not material. They cannot be touched, but they are real. If justice is not real, then the arbitrary killing of innocent children is not wrong, which is absurd. If love is nothing but *impulse, environmental conditioning, and subconscious drives, then to say, "I love you" is meaningless. If all our actions are predetermined, then they are not really our actions at all: I am not free to declare my love to you. Indeed, it is not even "I" who am speaking to you, but merely an impersonal event of matter and energy.

Matter is everything that can that is: meaning

ASK YOURSELF:
Is what I seek to know everything that in any way exists? Does it include such immeasurable things as thought, justice, and free choice? If so, it is reality I am seeking to know.

"The greatest and highest truths have no outward image of themselves visible to man. Immaterial things, which are the noblest and the greatest, are shown only in thought and idea, and in no other way."

Plato
Statesman 286a

Matter

All that is measurable

Matter includes only that which can be explored and measured by science. Science combines mathematics and experiment, considering only things that are quantifiable and ultimately verifiable by sense experience.

Because matter is real and can be known, I am perfectly justified in using the scientific method to investigate it. The complex interchange of matter and energy can be measured and formulated, and it should be. The scientific method has been successful in increasing our *knowledge of the material universe and in advancing technology, with its benefits for our safety, health, and comfort. The study of material reality is a worthy enterprise.

The various sciences study the material world. Biology studies the material reality of living organisms. Chemistry explains things in terms of chemical compositions. Physics explains these chemical compositions in terms of their constituent parts: atoms and subatomic particles. Because such things as ideas, *justice, *love, and *freedom of *choice are not material, science has no access to them. If we assume that science is our only access to *reality, we must logically deny that such things as ideas, justice, love, freedom of choice, and even the scientific method are real.

be measured; reality is everything as well as matter.

"Science starts,
not from large assumptions,
but from particular facts
discovered by observation
or experiment."

Bertrand Russell
Religion and Science, Ch. 1

ASK YOURSELF:
Is what I seek to know verifiable by science or the senses? Does it include only what can be weighed and measured? If so, it is matter that I am seeking to know.

Reason

Rules and content of thought

Reason is more than just logic: it also has insight into the various dimensions of *reality. It discovers *truth (the ways things are), prompts *goodness (the way things ought to be), and appreciates beauty (the harmonious order in things).

Reason grasps first principles and understands what can be deduced from these principles. The most basic truths, obligations, and aesthetic intuitions are the first principles of reason. The fact that something cannot be and not be at the same time and in the same respect is a first principle of truth. That I should never intentionally do what I know to be wrong is a first principle of *moral obligation. And it is a first principle of beauty that a beautiful thing is a unified and harmonious integration of parts within a whole.

By combining logic with insight into reality, reason reveals the meaningfulness of our being here. Reason helps us understand the world around us. When we try to explain our experiences, we are guided by a concern to avoid contradiction. Reason also helps us live moral lives. When we consider a course of action, we know we should choose what we know to be good and turn away from what we know is bad. Reason helps us appreciate beautiful things. We distinguish what is harmoniously unified from what is disordered.

Logic gives coherence to thought; reason meaningful world full of

ASK YOURSELF:
*Am I concerned with
the content as well as
the structure of thought?
Does my thought provide
insight into reality, obligation,
or beauty? If so, I am using
reason, not merely logic.*

*"He who will not reason is a bigot;
he who cannot is a fool;
he who dares not is a slave."*

William Drummond
Academical Question: Preface

Logic

Rules of thought

Logic has no content. It is merely the rules of correct reasoning. Logic is necessary for rational discussions, but it does not tell us what the discussions are about. In itself, logic does not reveal anything about *truth, *goodness, or beauty.

Logic assumes first principles and shows what follows from them. Thus, knowing that it is impossible for something to be and not be at the same time and in the same respect, logic shows me that paint cannot be both black and not black at the same time and in the same respect. Knowing that it is wrong intentionally to kill the innocent, logic shows me I should not kill this innocent person. Knowing that a beautiful object is an integrated whole, logic shows me that this jumble of sound is not beautiful.

We use logic every day, usually without having to seek out first principles. If we are hungry and food is available at home, we conclude that we should go home to eat. If we know that we are supposed to stop at red lights, we conclude that we should stop at this particular red light. If we have learned by experience that fire burns, we decide not to put our hand in this fire. If we know that *courage is better than *cowardice, we try to be courageous. All these particular conclusions follow logically from what we know already.

---

embraces logic, but also opens up a truth, goodness, and beauty.

"Logic is a machine of the mind, and if it is used honestly it ought to bring out an honest conclusion."

G. K. Chesterton
Varied Types, 113

ASK YOURSELF:
Am I concerned merely with the structure of thought? Does my thought simply avoid contradiction without providing insight? If so, I am exercising the logical dimension of reason.

Reform

The remaking of an existing order

As the word implies, reform is "forming again." Thus, in its root meaning, reform is a reordering. This implies a vision or plan, for we cannot form or reform something without a model.

Reform is a necessary feature of our continuing human communities. Because we are imperfect, our cooperative human endeavors — whether *friendships or institutions — tend toward decay. In order to preserve them, we must engage in ongoing reform. Thus, reform is justified, not just by the new vision, but by the old as well. If I am interested in reform, it is because I think that the present state of things has not lived up to the ideal. I want to remake the new in the image of what was best in the old. I wish to preserve what is *good in the old order while making it better.

If we wish to reform our government, we look to the constitutional ideals that have been lost, and we try to recapture them. If we want to reform a sports program, we consider the fundamental goods that such programs should embody (such as good sportsmanship and *fair competition) and try to bring them back into our program. In reforming our personal behavior, we look to those *moral ideals that we know deep down inside are worth following. We try to reform our *character by living up to these ideals.

Reform is change for the sake of perfecting
the sake of overthrowing that order or

∽

ASK YOURSELF:
*Is this change
aimed at improving
the present order?
Will this be achieved
by preserving what is
best in that order? If so,
the change is reform.*

*"Reform is a metaphor for reasonable
and determined men: it means that
we see a certain thing out of shape;
we mean to put it into shape;
and we know what shape."*

G. K. Chesterton
Orthodoxy, Ch. 7

Rebellion

The rejection of an existing order

As the word implies, rebellion is "fighting again" (*bellum* in Latin means "war"). Thus, in its root meaning, rebellion is a disordering. For this, no plan or vision is required.

Unlike reform, rebellion is not a necessary event in the process of human affairs. Given ongoing reform, there is no obvious reason why we should abandon the cooperative human institutions we have inherited. Thus, rebellion requires a justification. It cannot be justified by an appeal to the old order, for that is rejected. My rebellion might be justified if my new vision is simply incompatible with the cooperative institutions as they now exist. However, it might be that I just feel like casting off the old order. Rebellion may have its roots in mere subjective discontent.

Rebellions are usually an extreme solution to *problems. If the old order is really beyond saving, rebellion may be justified; but usually reform is possible, and preferable because it is less violent. Rebellions in government may be extremely cruel; consider the bloodbath of the French Revolution. Rebellions in general are often without vision and purpose beyond throwing off *authority. Sometimes, we rebel just to show our independence of social structures and (more dangerously) of *moral *laws.

---

an existing order; rebellion is change for perhaps only for the sake of change.

"Revolution is like a forest fire;
it burns everything in its path."

Malcolm X
*"Message to the Grass Roots," speech
in Detroit, 10 November 1963*

ASK YOURSELF:
Is this change aimed at overthrowing the present order? Will this be achieved by rejecting everything about that order? If so, the change is rebellion.

135

Respect

Deference paid to a good person

Respect depends primarily on *reason. The person we respect stands for what we know to be right. It is not a matter of finding the person pleasant or *useful. What matters is the person's *commitment to good.

When I respect someone, my focus is on that person's good *character and *wisdom. My respect continues whether or not the person is present. I am confident that this person will continue to be good and wise. For this reason, my respect can serve as a *moral guide for my own actions. The qualities in this person's character that I respect are universal. I see that they are good for that person, for me, and for all human beings.

Many of our relations with other people involve respect. We respect the teacher who makes us work hard (even though we might not enjoy the work) so long as the teacher is *fair and works hard too. We respect social workers for giving of their time and energy to help others. We respect the classmate who will not give in to peer pressure, but befriends the unpopular student. In every case, we respect the person who upholds the values that we know to be good and that we think everybody should uphold. Thus, respect always has an objective foundation in moral *goodness.

To fear someone is to have a subjective concern
to have an objective appreciation

ASK YOURSELF:
*Do I show a
special regard for
this person? Is my
regard due to the per-
son's commitment to
what is good? If so, my
regard is based on respect.*

*"Respect is actually the awareness
of a value to which even my
self-love must give way."*

Immanuel Kant
*Foundations of the Metaphysics
of Morals, Sect. 1, fn. 2*

Fear

Deference paid to a powerful person

Fear depends primarily on emotion. The person we fear stands in the way of our comfort. *Reason comes into play, but its role is secondary. We fear *pain and know that the person could cause us pain.

When I fear someone, the focus of my fear is a concern for my safety. Fear continues only so long as the person I fear is present or is close enough to be a real threat. I am afraid either of present danger or of the unpredictability of someone's behavior. The reasons for my fear are particular — this person in this situation with this power. If the situation changes or the person's *power is lost, my fear may disappear.

In many cases our relations with others are colored by fear. We fear the bully, partly because of his power to do us harm, but also because his actions are unpredictable. We may fear the unfair boss at work for the same reasons. Sometimes, we may even fear a just *authority. But when we do, we do not fear the *justice (which is an object of respect); rather, we fear the pain and humiliation we may suffer if our wrongdoing is discovered and *punished. In every case, fear is a subjective response to someone or something that causes or threatens to cause pain.

---

for our own safety, but to respect someone is for that person's goodness.

"He that fears you when present, will hate you when absent."

Thomas Fuller
Gnomologia (1732), No. 2101

⋙

ASK YOURSELF:
*Do I show a
special regard for this
person? Is my regard due
to a desire to avoid being
harmed by this person?
If so, my regard is based
on fear, not respect.*

Responsibility

Reasonable obligation and opportunity

A responsibility is something we *morally ought to do. It is negative, for it rules out certain actions. But it is also positive — an invitation to exercise *freedom of *choice in ways we know to be *good.

Key to a responsibility is that, although I may be given it by another, it is in some sense self-imposed. Responsibility (literally "the ability to respond") is a sign of *maturity. It presupposes that I have the ability to *think, to *judge, and to choose and that I can know what I should do. Thus, responsibility is not only an obligation for me, but also an opportunity to promote what I understand to be worthwhile. Responsibility presupposes the most essential kind of freedom: freedom of choice. This is the freedom to participate actively in *community.

Opportunities to be responsible are all around us. We have responsibilities within our families to work in appropriate ways for the good of all members. In sports or business, we have responsibilities to work for the success of the team. We all have responsibilities to *friends — to support them when they need help, to promote their *happiness, and to foster mutual giving. Understood properly, each of these responsibilities is an opportunity to grow in maturity by cooperating with others.

The burden of a responsibility is also freedom; the burden of a

ASK YOURSELF:
*Is this something
that I know I
should do? Is it
an opportunity to
exercise my freedom
of choice? If so, I
face a responsibility.*

"Each person has a name that no other can bear. There is a beauty, a strength, and a glory that each person has of his own. The whole universe is thrown out of kilter when you shrink from your magnanimous responsibility."

Herman Watts
"What Is Your Name?" in Philpot, ed., Best Black Sermons

Restriction

Limitation and loss of opportunity

A restriction is something that limits what we can do. It is, in itself, merely negative. Unlike responsibility, restriction is not simultaneously a positive invitation to exercise free *choice.

A restriction lacks the self-imposed characteristic of responsibility. Rather than being a sign of *maturity, a restriction is generally a sign of *servility. Its imposition makes me more like a servant or child who is forced to do things than a mature person who shoulders responsibility. A restriction involves a limitation of my social or *political *freedom — that is, a restriction of my freedom from outside interference. Although such freedom is not as essential to me as freedom of choice, it is nevertheless a *good that ought not to be curtailed without sufficient reason.

Restrictions on our freedom come from a number of sources, some just, some unjust. The rules parents impose on their teenage children are restrictive, but not unjust. Traffic laws are restrictive, but justly so, for they impose order for the safety and well-being of all. A coach's or employer's policy that limits opportunities for advancement on the basis of favoritism is an unjust restriction. Although restrictions may be unwanted and sometimes even unwarranted, they can be opportunities for *patience and *courage.

---

an opportunity to exercise mature
restriction is mere limitation.

"The mind of man
naturally hates everything
that looks like a restraint upon it."

Joseph Addison
The Spectator, 23 June 1712

ASK YOURSELF:
Is this something
that has been
forced on me? Is
it a limitation on
my freedom to do
as I please? If so, I
face a restriction.

Reverence

Respect for the being and goodness of things

Reverence rejoices in things' being what they are. To this extent, it is intimately bound up with *truth. Reverence also appreciates value, respecting each thing for being what it is, investing each with due *honor.

Reverence values things appropriately. If I am reverent, I respect things according to their intrinsic *goodness. Stones, birds, and persons are all worthy of reverence, but there is an objective hierarchy of goodness among them: people are to be revered more than birds, and birds more than stones. If I revere birds or stones more than I revere people, then I am wrong. Reverence is open to the goodness of all things, but not indiscriminately.

Since reverence is the appropriate *respect for all things, it applies to all our relations. A certain reverence is due even stones. The most coherent basis for environmental protection is that all things are worthy of reverence: persons, animals, plants, and even mountains and streams. Of course, some are more worthy than others, and so we must not sacrifice human lives for pristine wilderness. Among our relations with people, more reverence is due our parents and elders than our siblings and *friends, for they deserve more who have given us more (life, education, a *political *community).

Reverence gives to all things the respect with a significance and

ASK YOURSELF:
Do I honor each thing for the wonder of its being? Do I give greater honor to things that are more worthy? If so, I am being reverent.

"There is a value inherent in every stone, in a drop of water, in a blade of grass, precisely as an entity which possesses its own being, which is such and not otherwise."

Dietrich and Alice von Hildebrand
The Art of Living, Ch. 1

Superstition

Respect for illusory powers behind things

Superstition invests things with powers they do not have. To this extent, it is cloaked in falsehood. Rather than respecting each thing for what it is, superstition gives to things more or less *honor than they deserve.

Superstition values things inappropriately. If I am superstitious, I do not care about things for their own *goodness, but for what they can do for me. Fearing the unknown, I may wish to enlist the powers of things to protect me. Perhaps I trust in magic to keep me safe or to give me power. If I think that a bird or a stone will provide me with more protection or power than a person will, I honor the bird or stone above the person.

Superstition can enter whenever we give more *respect to something or someone than is due. To invest the earth with intelligence and *moral will and then to worship it is superstition. To think that it matters which side of the bed I get out of is also superstition. It is superstitious to rely on a good-luck charm. Again, it comes down to *truth and appropriate valuation. There is no reason to believe that the earth or sun is alive in the sense that we are alive. There is no reason to think that how we get out of bed affects our future. There is no reason to trust a good-luck charm.

---

they deserve; superstition invests some things
power they do not have.

~

*"It is our duty to eradicate superstition.
For superstition dogs our heels at every turn.
When you regard an omen, go to an
astrologer or fortune teller, or when some
prodigy appears, superstition is at your side."*

Cicero
Divination, Bk. 2, ch. 72

ASK YOURSELF:
*Do I honor things
according to my needs
and desires rather than
their worthiness? Do I give
some things greater honor
than they deserve? If so,
I am being superstitious.*

Right

What we may justly claim

A right is a legitimate claim to something. A right can be reasonably claimed only against those who can honor it (i.e., other persons), and a claim is legitimate only if it is justified *morally. Every right has its basis in some *good that should be honored.

If I can legitimately claim a right from others, I must honor the same right for others in my position. Every right comes with an obligation. If I have a universal right to be treated *fairly, I have an obligation to treat every other human being fairly. Not only do I have an obligation to honor the rights of others; I must also live in such a way that I honor the good that is the basis for the rights that I claim. Thus, if I have a right to safety when I drive my car, I have an obligation to honor the good of life by driving safely myself.

Our legal system guarantees a number of rights, most of which have their foundation in the natural moral law. We have a right to life and the protections necessary to ensure this, a right to an education, a right to own property, a right to a fair trial if we are accused of wrongdoing, and a right to the fruits of our labor, to name a few. Every one of these rights can be justified by *reason, and each carries with it an obligation on our part to honor the same right for others.

A right is a reasonable claim to some real
deserve; a want is an arbitrary claim to

ASK YOURSELF:
*Is what I desire
something to which
I have a legitimate
claim? Are others
obligated to honor
my desire? If so,
it is a right.*

*"We hold these truths to be self-evident;
that all men are created equal;
that they are endowed by their
creator with inalienable rights;
that among these are life, liberty,
and the pursuit of happiness."*

Thomas Jefferson
Declaration of Independence

Want

What we would like to have

A want is an arbitrary claim to something. A want cannot be reasonably claimed against others, since it is simply what we desire, not what is morally justified. A want can be for anything. But, since it is not based in a moral *good, the want need not be honored.

We may think we deserve to have our wants satisfied, but they are not guaranteed us by *morality. Wants may be universal, as are the desires for comfort and *pleasure, or they may be as particular as any whim. In neither case are they owed us. No mere want implies an obligation. Although someone may be obliged to give me what I need or deserve, no one is obliged to give me what I want. If society were obliged to give me everything I want, it would be obliged to do the same for every other *citizen. This is clearly absurd.

When a want corresponds to a fundamental good, we have a right to have it satisfied. For example, we want to live, to know the *truth, and to be treated *fairly, and we have a corresponding right to life, education, and *justice before the *law. However, wants are not limited to fundamental goods. When our wants are arbitrary, we have no right to have them satisfied. Perhaps, I want to be a millionaire, or a movie star, or president. No one has any obligation to give me these things.

---

good that all in the same circumstance
fulfillment of our particular desire.

*"If everyone can claim that any
felt want or need or longing is a right,
there are clearly no such things as rights
left at all, and we no longer have
any way of deciding what is a right
and what is not."*

Henry Fairlie
The Seven Deadly Sins Today, p. 93

ASK YOURSELF:
Is what I desire something I would like to have but cannot legitimately claim? Are others free from the obligation to honor my desire? If so, it is a want, not a right.

Ruler

One who orders others for their own good

The ruler's purpose is to employ his *authority to assure the well-being of others. The job of a ruler is not to impose his will, but to bring the good of *justice to the *community. A good ruler always has in mind what is best for the community.

The ruler's job is to serve the people. As a ruler, I ensure the security and material prosperity of those I serve. This means making sure that people are not cheating or killing one another. However, in addition to this external role of ensuring that people do not harm each other, I also am concerned that people be as *virtuous as possible. Obviously, I cannot make anyone good, for *moral *goodness is a matter of free *choice. However, I can be of help by setting a good example and by encouraging good institutions.

A good ruler may be found in all communal aspects of our lives. Within the family, a good parent orders the lives of the children so that they may learn to be good. The parent tries to help the child move from the pursuit of *pleasure to *responsible action. Community groups, sports teams, and businesses flourish under one who is *wise enough and caring enough to organize people so that they work together for mutual benefit. Of course, good rulers in government devote themselves to the well-being of those they serve.

A ruler's talents and power are bent
is intent on using the people to

≈

ASK YOURSELF:
*Does this person govern others for their benefit?
Is he concerned with their material and moral well-being?
If so, he is a ruler.*

"The object of government is the welfare of the people. The material progress and prosperity of a nation are desirable chiefly so far as they lead to the moral and material welfare of all good citizens."

Theodore Roosevelt
The New Nationalism (1910)

Tyrant

One who orders others for his own good

The tyrant's purpose is to employ his *power to get what he wants. He is not concerned with the well-being of those in his power. Rather, the tyrant imposes his will for his own sake. He is motivated by self-interest and not by the good of the *community.

The tyrant serves himself. As a tyrant, my main concern is to ensure the security and material prosperity of myself. If this is achieved by getting the people to live virtuously, I will try to instill *virtue in the people. But if this can be done more simply and with greater rewards for me by intimidating the people or even getting them to fight among themselves, this is what I will do. As a tyrant, I seek to maximize my own power, prestige, *wealth, and *pleasure. I use the people to fulfill this purpose.

Tyrants can be found wherever there is opportunity for domination. Within a family, that parent is a tyrant who lays down the law merely to assert his power, without regard to what is really best for the children. When a coach or CEO is interested only in control and personal success, she is a tyrant. And of course, it is possible to have tyrants in government, such as Hitler. Groups of people (the rich, a particular party) or even the majority of people can also be tyrannical if they are motivated by desire and power, not *justice.

---

on serving those who are ruled; a tyrant
serve his own self-interested desires.

"Tyranny at last becomes a disease. . . .
The man and the citizen disappear
forever in the tyrant."

Fyodor Dostoyevsky
The House of the Dead (Prison Life
in Siberia), Part 1, ch. 9

ASK YOURSELF:
Does this person
govern others for his own
benefit? Is he concerned
only for his material well-
being, ignoring the welfare
of those under him? If
so, he is a tyrant.

Self-control

Moderation of bodily desires

Self-control is the ability to deal with *pleasure in a reasonable way. Desire is ordered for the sake of the entire human being. Self-control is a fundamental *virtue, allowing us to live according to *reason and *freedom, not *impulse.

My self-control is clearly good for society (because it prevents me from harming others by acting on my passions), but it is also good for me. It allows me to choose my actions rather than having circumstances determine my actions. Self-control does not deny my animal nature by suppressing my appetites; rather, it gives proper play to all aspects of my being — reason, emotions, and appetites. If I let my appetites and emotions run wild, I invite anarchy and discord, for they are many and each demands immediate gratification.

A classic example of self-control involves our sexual impulses. These are obviously natural. But if not controlled, they will lead to anarchy in the *community (rape, uncared-for children, venereal disease, and AIDS) and disorder in the individual. Self-control helps us moderate our eating and drinking. And it prevents us from being overcome by such emotions as anger and *fear. Self-control allows us freely to choose what to do based on reason, rather than responding to nonrational urges and appetites.

Whereas repression rejects all orders them for the good

ASK YOURSELF:
Do I refuse to let bodily pleasure run my life? Do I order my participation in bodily pleasure appropriately? If so, I am exercising self-control.

"The appetites must be made subject to the control of reason, and not allowed to run ahead of it or to lag behind. Then will strength and character and self-control shine through in all their brilliance."

Cicero
On Moral Obligation, Bk. 1, ch. 29

Repression

Rejection of bodily desires

Repression is the unreasonable rejection of sensual *pleasure. Whereas self-control orders desire, repression tries to extinguish it. Far from being a *virtue, repression inhibits the exercise of *reason and *freedom.

To repress all desire for pleasure is bad for me and for society. As a bodily being, I naturally desire pleasure. Repression tries to deny my bodily nature. This is clearly bad for me, for I am an animal: to deny this is in some way to deny my very self. Since the attempt to reject my animal nature is doomed to failure, it inevitably leads to frustration. My frustration and unhappiness, in turn, disrupt my relations with others. Thus, to repress all bodily desires violates what reason tells me is a properly human life in *community.

Repression of bodily desires may lead to psychological and physical problems. Responding to some pleasures is strictly necessary for my survival — eating and drinking, for example. Repression of these desires may cause serious physical harm, as in the case of anorexia. And whereas *chastity is an example of self-control, repressing sexual desire cuts us off from a natural orientation toward communion with other human beings. Our sensual desires need to be ordered by reason, not be obliterated.

---

bodily pleasures, self-control of others and ourselves.

"If there be someone who finds nothing pleasurable, that person would be far from being human. The temperate person loves pleasures as right reason dictates."

Aristotle
Nicomachean Ethics, Bk. 3, ch. 14

ASK YOURSELF:
Do I refuse to let bodily pleasure run my life? Do I reject all participation in bodily pleasure? If so, I am repressing, not controlling, my desires.

147

Self-examination

Finding the world in ourselves

Self-examination is reflection on our knowledge of the world and on our *choices and actions in the world. By becoming aware of ourselves as knowers and *moral agents, we learn through self-examination how to find the *truth about *reality and how to be reasonable in our actions.

Self-examination is not a once-in-a-lifetime achievement, but an ongoing activity of discovery. It is inclusionary — simultaneously my discovery of a meaningful world and of my own ability and *responsibility to act in that world. It means being conscious of my *judgments, both about the way things are and about what I should do. Self-examination leads me to deeper understanding and better choices. As such, it is good for me and good for the *community.

Self-examination involves asking myself a number of *questions, some general and some specific. What is life all about? Why do I do wrong? How could I lead a better life? What is the nature of thought and free choice? Have I been thorough in considering this particular question? Did I get my facts right? How should this particular person be treated in this particular situation? These are the questions that lead to self-knowledge.

Self-examination reflects on the self in order
self-absorption turns inward, ignoring

ASK YOURSELF:
*Do I question what
I am thinking and
doing? Are my questions
inspired by a desire to
know what really is true
and good? If so, my quest
is self-examination.*

*"The unexamined life
is not worth living."*

Socrates
In Plato's Apology 38a

148

Self-absorption

Losing the world in ourselves

Self-absorption is a turning inward, away from the world. We seek to know the isolated self and look to do what this isolated self feels like doing. But isolated from objective *reality and purpose, the self has very little content. So nothing seems real, and nothing seems worth doing.

My self-absorption puts an end to the process of discovery. Unlike self-examination, it is exclusionary. Rather than trying to understand myself in the contexts of a meaningful world and a moral *community, I focus on myself alone. Appearance replaces reality — the way I want to be replaces the way I am. *Feeling replaces *morality — how I feel like acting replaces the *choice to do what is best. Self-absorption leads me further from reality. It is bad for me and bad for the *community.

Self-absorption severely limits the kinds of *questions I ask, since I am not concerned about my relation to a real world with real other people. When I do ask questions, they are distorted by my preoccupation with myself. Why is my life so difficult? Why are people always unfair to me? How come nobody understands me? These questions lead, not to self-knowledge, but to alienation from self and community.

---

to know better what is true and good;
questions of what is true and good.

"The true value of a human being
is determined primarily by the measure
and the sense in which he has attained
liberation from the self."

Albert Einstein
The World as I See It (1931)

ASK YOURSELF:
*Do I think only
about what I am think-
ing and doing? Are my
thoughts unrelated to
what is objectively true
and good? If so, I am
self-absorbed.*

Self-respect

Appropriate regard for ourselves

Since every human (ourselves included) deserves respect, self-respect is not only permissible but obligatory. It should, however, be based on a true evaluation of our own worth.

Self-respect is foundational for my own *happiness and for my effective participation in the world. Self-respect indicates that I take myself seriously as a person with *freedom and *responsibility, as opposed to a mere animal driven by instinct and the desire for *pleasure. Such intelligent freedom is a key ingredient in happiness. Self-respect also gives me the confidence to participate effectively in many dimensions of the *community. Without self-respect, I fail to enter into meaningful relationships of *equality with others.

Self-respect is a positive support for many of our activities. Without sufficient self-respect, we do not believe in ourselves enough to contribute effectively to a sports team or theater project. In order to progress academically, we need to respect ourselves as intelligent agents. Success in the various vocations of life — business, medicine, teaching, etc. — requires that we regard ourselves as worthy of contributing in these cooperative ventures. Only if we respect ourselves as worthy of being loved and able to love can true *friendship develop.

Self-respect honors our true nature as a being
rests on the false judgment that

"Oft times nothing profits more Than self-esteem, grounded on just and right."

John Milton
Paradise Lost, Bk. 8, l. 572

Self-satisfaction

Exaggerated regard for ourselves

Since no human (ourselves included) is perfect, no one should be satisfied with his present state. The caution against self-satisfaction is based on a true evaluation of our own worth.

Self-satisfaction is a chain that prevents me from acting effectively in the world and also from achieving personal *happiness. If I think that I am perfect as I am, I will not bother to try to be more *just and *truthful and kind. Wrapped up in myself, I will not participate in the building of a *community of mutual *respect. Self-satisfaction also prevents me from pursuing many key ingredients in happiness — developing my talents, expanding my understanding of *reality, and ordering my *moral life by intelligent *choice.

Self-satisfaction has a negative effect on many aspects of our lives. If we are self-satisfied, we will not contribute to a sports team or theater company to our full potential. Self-satisfaction stifles our academic progress, for if we think we have all the answers, we cannot learn. Nor will we succeed in the various jobs of life if we think that we need no further improvement. Most obviously, real *friendship is impossible if we are self-satisfied, for it kills the spirit of giving. Mutual giving is just as necessary as mutual respect in creating fruitful relationships.

---

endowed with reason and free will; self-satisfaction
we are sufficiently wise and good.

⤳

*"What is the first business of philosophy?
To part with self-conceit. For it is impossible
for anyone to begin to learn what
he thinks that he already knows."*

Epictetus
Applying General Principles to Particular Cases, 17

ASK YOURSELF:
*Do I value myself
just for being me?
Does this valuation
interfere with my
intellectual and moral
improvement? If so, it
is self-satisfaction.*

Simplicity

Having the moral innocence of a child

Simplicity is a matter of the will. It is to be pure in our intention: *honest, innocent of conniving, and trusting. Simplicity means being open to and grateful for the gifts that the world brings to us. Simplicity is characteristic of young children.

Such a quality should never be put aside — not by popular teenagers, not by powerful politicians, not by parents teaching children. For without simplicity, *community is impossible. Communal life depends on straightforwardness and trust. *Friendship requires that I believe your profession of loyalty. Any cooperative venture — school, business, sports — relies on trust. Without a simple openness and the willingness to learn, I can make no progress in *knowledge or *virtue, for I can learn only when I have the *humility to admit that I do not have all the answers.

To understand the *goodness of simplicity, consider young children. They are not weighed down by *prejudice or cynicism. They do not care about race or social or economic status. They greet each other with a willingness to trust and befriend. Simplicity is found in a child's capacity to *hope and to *wonder. Children are always ready to try again, never losing hope in the fulfillment of their dreams. They are full of *questions and eager to learn.

Simplicity wills no evil, gives thanks, and recognize the dangers of evil and

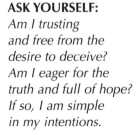

ASK YOURSELF:
*Am I trusting
and free from the
desire to deceive?
Am I eager for the
truth and full of hope?
If so, I am simple
in my intentions.*

*"Beauty of style and harmony and grace
and good rhythm depend on the true
simplicity of a rightly and nobly
ordered mind and character, not
that other simplicity which is
only a euphemism for folly."*

Plato
Republic, Bk. 3, 400b

Foolishness

Having the intellectual weakness of a child

Foolishness is a matter of the intellect. It is to be unduly influenced by *feelings and fancy rather than by *reason. To be foolish is to have poor *judgment. Because their minds are undeveloped, foolishness is characteristic of young children.

Such a quality should be put aside as soon as possible — although we accept it in young children. My foolishness is not good for me, nor is it good for others. If I am foolish, I make poor decisions. I follow passion instead of reason; I cannot foresee the consequences of my acts. If I am foolish, I can easily be duped. This is bad not only for me, but for society as a whole. My foolishness in some sense encourages others to take advantage of me. More generally, for me to act foolishly will prevent me from helping others; and it may even result in my hurting them.

To understand the dangers of foolishness, consider young children. They act on *impulse rather than following sound judgment. They do things that turn out to be harmful to them or to others, because they are unable to foresee consequences. Their powers of discrimination are weak, so they are unable to judge who should be trusted and who should not. It would be a grave mistake for us to imitate the foolishness of children along with their innocence.

---

trusts in goodness; foolishness fails to
follows impulse rather than reason.

*"The more a mind is empty
and without counterpoise,
the more easily it gives
beneath the weight of the
first persuasive argument."*

Montaigne
Essays, Bk.1, ch. 27

ASK YOURSELF:
*Am I guided by
impulse rather than
by reason? Am I
unable or unwilling
to make wise choices?
If so, I am foolish
in my judgments.*

Sophistication

Real cultivation of intellect and manners

A sophisticated person knows how to deal with many kinds of people and situations with *honesty and *politeness. This is because the sophisticated person looks up to the principles of *truth and *virtue that are above all people.

Sophistication leads to a deepening of *character and is the product of *patience and effort. If I am sophisticated, I understand through what I have done, seen, and experienced that the particularities of a person's background, ancestry, and cultural opportunities do not matter essentially. I am able to transcend the differences that divide me from other people and find those common grounds that unite us as human beings.

The sophisticated person is able to put anyone at ease. She can make conversation as easily with the President of the United States and the local gas-station attendant as she can with her circle of close friends. Because of her vast experience and the breadth of her education, she can walk into a room full of strangers and find something to talk about with each person. And because she understands the difference between a person's quality and social status, she is able to appreciate and encourage real talent and accomplishment in others.

Real sophistication makes a person wiser pretense of wisdom and generosity,

ASK YOURSELF:
*Have education
and experiences
made this person
more open-minded?
Does he put rich and
poor equally at ease?
If so, he is sophisticated.*

*"The gentle mind by gentle deeds is known.
For a man by nothing is so well bewrayed
As by his manners."*

Edmund Spenser
Fairie Queene, Bk. 6, canto 3, st. 1

Snobbishness

Fake cultivation of intellect and manners

A snob puts on a façade of not caring in order to appear to be above people and situations. Rather than looking up to principles, the snob looks down on people, making use of his knowledge to put people in their places.

Snobbishness leads to a narrowing of *character and is the product of a negativity that is easy to adopt. As a snob, I think that I am better simply because of what I have done, seen, and experienced. I think that those who have not had my privileged opportunities are somehow of less value. Since I am so concerned about the particular differences between me and others, I am unable to communicate with others on an equal footing.

The snob has a way of making everyone ill at ease. Not only does he treat the gas-station attendant rudely, but he also looks down upon those who rival his social position. Thus, a snob who graduated from Harvard considers himself superior to people who graduated from Yale, and vice versa. The snob reduces all to social status, equating the quality of a person with that person's background, *wealth, or connections. In this way, the snob fails to recognize and appreciate real talent and accomplishment when he sees it.

---

and more generous; snobbishness, the mere makes a person silly and selfish.

"The true snob never rests; there is always a higher goal to attain, and there are, by the same token, always more and more people to look down upon."

Russell Lynes
Snobs (1950)

ASK YOURSELF:
Have education and experiences made this person proud? Does he put down all those who are not the same as he? If so, he is a snob.

Stability

Lack of change where change is bad

Stability is consistency of activity that supports a vital order. Biologically, it is health. Psychologically, it is sanity. Morally, it is a confirmed *commitment to a life of *virtue.

Stability tends to fruitfulness. If my health is stable, I am able to perform many physical actions easily, but I can also turn my attention to other things. The same is true of psychological stability; it allows me to interact in a productive way with my environment and with other people. The *moral stability of virtue enables me to interact freely within a *community, but also, by calming my passions and ordering my life, it allows me to turn my attention to other pursuits, such as science and art.

Consider a few examples of the fruitfulness of stability in the moral sphere. Stability in *friendship not only allows the friendship to grow; it also offers friends the structure and support they need to pursue other meaningful activities. The same is true of the stability provided by marriage. The knowledge of mutual commitment in love allows each spouse the *freedom to develop while providing a stable home for children. To be a member of a stable community is to receive the benefits of protection, comfort, and intellectual challenge and support.

The consistency of stability is the the consistency of stagnation

∽

ASK YOURSELF:
Is the consistency in question natural and beneficial? Does it provide a platform for further growth and enrichment? If so, it is stability.

"A party of order or stability, and a party of progress are both necessary elements of a healthy state of political life."

J. S. Mill
Principles of Political Economy (1848),
"A Treatise on Flemish Husbandry"

Stagnation

Lack of change where change is good

Stagnation is consistency of inactivity that destroys a vital order. Biologically, it is illness. Psychologically, it is boredom. Morally, it is a lack of motivation to be *virtuous.

Stagnation tends to barrenness. The biological stagnation of illness makes me unable to perform many physical functions and may cause me to be preoccupied with my body to the exclusion of other pursuits. The psychological stagnation of boredom wastes my opportunities to learn about and participate in the world around me and may cause me to turn inward in *self-absorption. The *moral stagnation of *indifference prevents me from living a meaningful life of generosity and *friendship.

Unlike stability, stagnation erodes moral *commitments. A stagnant *friendship is one in which friends are no longer alive to the changes in each other, nor making the effort to find new common ground; such a friendship ceases to grow and begins to unravel. The same is true of a stagnant marriage. Spouses inevitably change as they grow older; if they are not alive to each other's changes and do not respond to them, the marriage will fail. A *community will fall apart if the goods of mutual protection, comfort, and intellectual support are taken for granted and ignored.

---

springboard to fruitful activity;
stifles activity and is barren.

*"Freedom is not an ideal,
it is not even a protection,
if it means nothing more than
the freedom to stagnate."*

Adlai Stevenson
Putting First Things First, Random House (1960)

ASK YOURSELF:
Is the consistency in question unnatural and harmful? Does it prevent the activities of growth and enrichment that should be flourishing? If so, it is stagnation, not stability.

Statesman

One who uses power for the good of people

A statesman is *wise and *just. Because he is wise, the statesman knows what is best for the *community and how to go about making his vision a reality. Because he is just, the statesman does what is best for the community as a whole.

A great statesman is able to motivate people to participate in his vision. If I am a great statesman, I am an excellent speaker and a good *leader. I appeal primarily to what is best in people — their *reason and conscience — by using sound arguments based on *truth and good *moral principles, but I can also make these truths attractive. I lead by example, living according to the principles I propose for the community. Preferring truth and *honesty to *power, I am not willing to use deception to preserve my position.

Great statesmen are rare, for it is difficult to hold to high moral principles and succeed in retaining power. Although not without flaws, a number of the founding fathers of our country were great statesmen. George Washington and Thomas Jefferson had a vision for their country based on truth and justice and were able, in large measure, to make this vision a reality. Abraham Lincoln insisted on the dignity of all human beings and worked for the reconciliation of a country stricken by civil war.

Both the statesman and the demagogue care about
uses power for the people, the

ASK YOURSELF:
Is this person able to move people to action? Is the action aimed at the good of the community? If so, the person is a statesman.

"The care of human life and happiness, and not their destruction, is the first and only legitimate object of good government."

Thomas Jefferson
To the Republican Citizens of
Washington County, Maryland

Demagogue

One who manipulates people to gain power

A demagogue is clever and self-interested. Because he is clever, the demagogue knows how to make his vision a reality. Because he is self-interested, his vision is centered on getting what he wants rather than on promoting what is best for the *community.

A successful demagogue is able to motivate people to accept his vision. If I am a demagogue, I am an excellent speaker and adept at getting people to do what I want. I appeal primarily to their passions and *prejudices, using half-truths, ambiguities, and even lies, if necessary, to preserve and augment my *power. I expect discipline and self-restraint in others (they should conform to my vision), but I exempt myself. *Truth and *honesty, if they get in the way, are sacrificed to my self-glorification in the eyes of the world.

The twentieth century gave us examples of demagogues. Hitler and Mussolini were highly successful speakers who were able to get people to follow them by appealing to spurious arguments of a master race and the destiny of a people. Joseph Stalin convinced people of the justice of mass exterminations for the Communist party. Saddam Hussein and Slobodan Milosevic are modern demagogues. They ensure their power by inflaming the passions and prejudices of one *group of people to destroy another.

---

people and power, but whereas the statesman demagogue uses people to get power.

"When states are democratically governed according to law, there are no demagogues; the best citizens are securely in the saddle; but when the laws are not sovereign, there you find demagogues."

Aristotle
Politics, Bk. 4, pt. 4

ASK YOURSELF:
Is this person able to move people to action? Is the action aimed at the empowerment and glorification of the person himself? If so, the person is a demagogue.

Student

Follower of truth

A student eagerly follows the *truth, wherever it may lead. A real student wants to know the truth for its own sake. It makes no difference to the student where the truth is to be found or who taught or teaches it.

To be a student is a noble thing in itself, for it is always good to seek the truth. As a student, I am clearly doing something of intrinsic value to myself: the more I know, the more fully I participate in *reality. But being a student is good not only for me; it is also good for society as a whole, and this in two ways. First, the more I know, the more I can share the truth with others. Second, my spirit of open inquiry — my eagerness and earnestness in the quest for truth — encourages the same spirit in others.

Every kind of truth is worth knowing. It is good to know how to speak other languages and to understand calculus. It is worth knowing the biological make-up of living things. It is good to know the truth about how we should lead our lives and to know as much as possible about the ultimate *mysteries of reality — the nature of thought and of *freedom and the cause of the universe. A good student is eager to know and, in participating in the many fields of *knowledge, does something intrinsically worthwhile.

A student follows truth and does
follows a person and

ASK YOURSELF:
Do I seek the truth for its own sake? Do I welcome truth no matter what the source? If so, I am a student.

"Dear to me is Plato, but dearer still the truth."

Aristotle
Nicomachean Ethics, Bk. 1

Disciple

Follower of a person

A disciple follows a person, wherever that person may lead. In itself, discipleship has no necessary connection with *truth. The charisma of the person matters more to the disciple than what the person teaches, whether true or false.

To be a disciple may or may not be a noble thing. It depends on the nobility of the person I follow and my reasons for following. Only if the person I follow teaches the truth about *reality and *morality is my discipleship objectively a good thing. Yet even if this is so, there can be wrong reasons for following a person. I may follow because the person is charismatic or because I love to see the person defeat others in rational argument. All of these reasons make my discipleship suspect.

Discipleship may be found wherever there is something to be learned. We may be disciples of masters in philosophy or in art or music. We may follow moral or spiritual masters. To the extent that the master has something of value to teach, discipleship can be a good thing. But there are twin dangers in following a person: first, if we follow a person who is imperfect, we will be, if not misled, at least limited; second, if we follow a person instead of the truth, we make truth a matter of secondary importance.

not care where it is found; a disciple so risks losing the truth.

"Disciples owe unto masters only a temporary belief and a suspension of their own judgement till they be fully instructed, and not an absolute resignation or perpetual captivity."

Francis Bacon
The Advancement of Learning, Bk. 1, ch. 4, sect. 12

ASK YOURSELF:
Do I seek to follow a person? Do I equate whatever the person teaches with truth? If so, I am a disciple.

Tenacity

Refusal to give up

Tenacity is the dedicated adherence to something we know to be worthwhile. As such, tenacity is positive. It involves a clear purpose — to persevere in what is *good — and welcomes new *evidence and perspectives that clarify or enrich that good.

Tenacity is particularly evident when the adherence required is difficult. If my perseverance requires great effort of body or mind, or if it requires me to face a great deal of peer pressure and perhaps even ridicule, then my holding fast to my good purpose shows strength of mind and *courage. In such cases, there may be little to gain in terms of social standing, but much in *moral standing. Tenaciously holding to what is *true and good not only benefits me in terms of *virtue; it also works to ensure the *stability of these goods in the *community.

The high school athlete who, on the first and second tries, does not make the varsity team, but who continues to work hard, finally gaining a place on the team, is tenacious. It requires tenacity to understand a difficult math concept or to succeed in interpreting a complicated poem. On the social and political levels, it takes tenacity and *patience to stick to our principles and persevere through long hours of work to make the community better.

Tenacity is a firm choice of the will guided choice of the will guided by the

ASK YOURSELF:
Is my refusal to yield based on an adherence to objective truth and objective value? Is there a rational clarity to my purpose? If so, I am being tenacious.

"Morale is a state of mind. It is steadfastness and courage and hope. It is confidence and zeal and loyalty. It is élan, esprit de corps, and determination."

General George C. Marshall

Stubbornness

Refusal to give in

Stubbornness is the uncompromising insistence on having our own way. As such, stubbornness is negative. It involves a kind of blindness, along with a willful rejection of *evidence and the perspectives of others.

Stubbornness is particularly evident when the compromise required is easy. If the evidence I need to convince me to change my mind is readily available, or if accepting another's perspective would mean giving up little of importance, then my refusal to yield is not reasonable, but is motivated by stubbornness. There is little to lose except my desire to be in control. Such rigid clinging to my own will hurts the *community, because I refuse to cooperate with others, and it also prevents me from becoming successful and *virtuous.

The young child who does not get his way and so throws a tantrum is stubborn. When we insist that our answer is correct, even when we know that we do not have all the evidence and that there may very well be other reasonable perspectives on the issue, we are being stubborn. Politically, we may be so stubborn in our *commitment to our particular cause or candidate that we shut down the process of evaluating issues and *character.

---

by objective value; stubbornness is a firm subjective desire to be right.

"Stubbornness and stupidity are twins."

Sophocles
Antigone, l. 1023

ASK YOURSELF:
Is my refusal to yield based on a desire to have things my way? Is there an irrational insistence to my purpose? If so, I am being stubborn.

Thinking

Knowing things

Thinking grasps the basic characteristics of a thing. It focuses on the essential elements a thing must have in order to be the kind of thing it is, leaving out of account all irrelevant particularities. Thinking gives us mental access to a thing's nature, which it shares with other things like it.

Thinking is necessary for science and *morality. If I remain on the level of particular images, I can never advance in my *knowledge of how the universe is ordered, for every sense image is particular; no two trees or rabbits look exactly the same. Although every situation is unique in time, place, and feeling, thought reveals to me the universal *truth that I should never kill an innocent person — regardless of the time, the place, or my feeling. My thinking draws universal truths from the particular things I experience.

By thinking, we know what things are — their essences. A pen can be blue and metallic or red and plastic. These qualities do not make it a pen. The essence of a pen is to be a writing instrument. A triangle is not necessarily scalene, equilateral, large, or small: it is a three-sided planar figure. The essence of a human being is not to be old or young, male or female, black or white; it is to be a rational animal. Thinking makes the natures of things clear to us.

Imagining presents the particularities of things to grasp the essential and

ASK YOURSELF:
Am I aware of the general characteristics of something? Do these characteristics reveal the kind of thing it is? If so, I am thinking, not imagining.

"Thinking is very hard and imagining is very easy and we are very lazy. We have fallen into the habit of using imagination as a crutch, and our intellects have almost lost the habit of walking."

Frank Sheed
Theology and Sanity, Ch. 2

Imagining

Picturing things

Imagination presents to us a picture of a thing in all its particularity. It is not able to present us with that which is essential about the thing. An image, either of direct sense or memory, is a prerequisite for thinking; but imagination is not sufficient to grasp a thing's nature.

Without images I would have no direct access to the things in the physical world around me; the images I sense or remember make my reflection on *reality possible. However, I must not think that the pictures in my imagination adequately indicate what is essential about the things I experience, for to do so is to fail to know the *truth. A plastic rose and a living rose might look the same, but they are essentially different. A black man and a white man may look different, but they are essentially the same.

Images that accompany thought are always particular. When I think about a pen or a triangle, a particular image (blue and plastic, equilateral) accompanies my thought. But I know the image is not what a pen or triangle is. Math helps us distinguish between thinking and imagination, for we can think about what a circle is (a planar figure with all points equidistant from one central point), but we cannot form an actual mental image of such a perfect form.

---

to us; thinking goes beyond particularities
universal natures of things.

ASK YOURSELF:
*Am I picturing the
particular characteristics
of something? Do these
characteristics pertain only
to this individual thing?
If so, I am imagining,
not thinking.*

Tolerance

Acceptance of a wide range of behavior

Tolerance is the willingness to accept actions we believe to be inappropriate or even wrong because it would be worse to take action against them. Tolerance is *community-oriented. Ideally, all bad behavior should cease, but it is unrealistic to think that society could succeed in enforcing this ideal. Tolerance understands this.

Determining what should and what should not be tolerated takes experience and *prudence. Every society must tolerate some wrongdoing, because the price of eliminating it might be greater than the price of allowing it. For example, so long as private wrongdoing does no serious harm to the public, tolerance is required; for the invasion of privacy necessary to correct every personal *fault would likely be worse than the fault itself.

However, it cannot be that serious wrongdoings should be tolerated for social order. Some situations warrant the toleration of some wrongdoing, but no situation makes every act permissible. We should, as a society, tolerate a certain amount of rudeness in the name of *free speech and arrogance in the name of individual expression. But to tolerate crimes such as rape and murder would be wrong, since tolerating them would do greater harm to the community than correcting them would.

Tolerance accepts some inappropriate behavior
denies that good has any universal

ASK YOURSELF:
*Do I accept some actions
that do not conform to
objective moral standards?
Is this because the attempt
to correct all faults would be
worse for the community? If so,
I am tolerant, not a relativist.*

*"I think that the state ought to
tolerate every principle of philosophy;
nor is there an instance, that any
government has suffered in its political
interests by such indulgence."*

David Hume
Concerning Human Understanding, Sect. 11, 114

Relativism

Acceptance of all behavior

Relativism is the assumption that there is no right or wrong. No action is considered better or worse than any other. If this is so, all actions are equally acceptable. Relativism is profoundly anti-community. If there are no standards of *morality to which we should adhere, tolerance is no better than intolerance.

Relativism cannot distinguish between more or less serious wrongdoing. If I am a relativist, I cannot (if I am to be consistent) praise or blame any moral position. If I blame you for some action, you could always reply that my *judgment is relative to my particular time, culture, upbringing, personality, etc., but not to yours. Since you are different from me in these respects, I cannot rightly criticize your action.

There are degrees of relativism. Ethics could be judged to be relative to a particular culture, era, economic class, gender, or *group. Ultimately, however, such group relativism tends to lead to individual relativism; for if there are no universal rights and wrongs, there is no reason why anyone in a certain group or culture should abide by the relative values of that group or culture. Tolerance arises out of a concern for the *community, but relativism rules out the possibility of common values and, hence, community.

---

for the sake of the common good; relativism meaning and so accepts all behavior.

⤳

"And are things relative to individuals, as Protagoras tells us? For he says that man is the measure of all things, and that things are to me as they appear to me, and that they are to you as they appear to you."

Plato
Cratylus 386a

ASK YOURSELF:
Do I refuse to pass judgment on any actions? Is this because I deny the existence of objective moral standards? If so, I am a relativist.

Tradition

The presence of the past

Tradition is living and meaningful precedence. It is the continuing influence of those who have gone before us. The reasons for this continuation may be merely habitual ("we have always done it this way") or because what is continued is good.

Tradition involves an attitude of openness, not just to what is new, but to what is true, good, and beautiful. If I find *truth, *goodness, and beauty in the works of those who have gone before me, I wish to enjoy these now and preserve them for the future. Since truth, goodness, and beauty have no specific temporal direction (unlike *progress in science and technology), it would be foolish of me to reject these elements of tradition just because they were brought into being in the past.

Traditions can be local or universal. A family might have a tradition of going to the same college or gathering together at special times. A *community might have a tradition of celebrating its founding with specific rituals. On a larger scale, there are intellectual and legal traditions that Western civilization has inherited from the Greeks and Romans. There are great religious traditions that enrich the lives of those who practice them. Of course, it is possible for a tradition to be *morally bad; such a tradition should be rejected.

The past, as past, is no more; tradition, is a rich resource of

⌇

ASK YOURSELF:
*Is this thing from
the past an active
part of the present?
Is it still relevant to
my present life?
If so, it is part
of a tradition.*

*"Tradition means giving votes to the
most obscure of all classes,
our ancestors. It is the
democracy of the dead."*

G. K. Chesterton
Orthodoxy, Ch. 4

The Past

The lost present

The past is mere temporal precedence. Every present moment is soon lost in the past. In strict temporal terms, the past is nothing at all. There are no good reasons to recover the past, and such a recovery is impossible.

If we equate what is *good with what is new, we are likely to consider the old as obsolete. We may *judge anything that is past with disdain. As I look around me and see the great *progress that has been made in science and technology, I might think of the past as merely primitive. I might think that we moderns have moved beyond the past. There is no need to think about it anymore. Let us use the present as a springboard for progress. Let us forget the past and simply focus on the future.

Considering the past in terms of its medicine, science, or technology, it is reasonable to pay it little thought. What is the point of using old methods of medicine when new ones work better? Why work with a Ptolemaic system when Copernicus and Einstein have so advanced our knowledge of the universe? Why build roads with shovels when we have bulldozers, or use typewriters when computers are much faster? There are good reasons to leave behind things that are not traditions but only obsolete elements of the past.

as the living presence of the past,
wisdom and culture.

"In the West the past is like a dead animal. It is a carcass picked at by the flies that call themselves historians and biographers. But in my culture the past lives."

Miriam Makeba
My Story (1987)

ASK YOURSELF:
Is this thing just an obsolete leftover from what has been? Is it irrelevant to my present life? If so, it is simply part of the temporal past.

Truth

Knowledge of reality

Truth is a success term. To know the truth is to know with *certainty that something exists or what something is. Truth is objective *knowledge, accessible to all *thinkers.

When I seek the truth, I expect that there is a right answer — the same for you, for me, and for everyone. Although we may not always agree about whether this or that particular claim is true, we do know that, if we are presented with the truth, we should both accept it. Thus, truth is something universally applicable, not something that depends on one individual's perspective. I know that a claim is true when there is clear and sufficient *evidence to support it.

Consider a few examples of truth. Mathematics provides a clear model: 2+2=4; a whole is greater than one of its parts. These propositions are absolutely clear and certain. We do not seek for more evidence. However, certainty is not confined to mathematics and logic. We know, for instance, that New York City is larger than Boston, and we know that *love is better than hate. Although certainty is harder to achieve for complicated problems of science and ethics, we all have access to the same basic theoretical and *moral truths.

Opinions are subjective perspectives on truth is objective certainty,

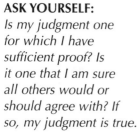

ASK YOURSELF:
Is my judgment one for which I have sufficient proof? Is it one that I am sure all others would or should agree with? If so, my judgment is true.

"To say of what is that it is, and of what is not that it is not, is to speak the truth."

Aristotle
Metaphysics, 1011b 24

Opinion

A perspective on reality

Opinions are either incomplete *knowledge or matters of taste. In neither case are opinions *certain and objective knowledge. Since opinions are subjective, they are not necessarily accessible to all.

When I hear someone's opinion, I am not expecting a complete explanation, irrefutably correct for him, for me, and for everyone. I ask for your opinion because I want to learn about your perspective, which may very well be different from my own. Opinions are not necessarily universally applicable. However, collecting various opinions is often the first step in finding the truth. A claim is still only an opinion when it lacks the support of clear and sufficient *evidence.

Opinions range from highly plausible accounts to mere matters of taste. The opinion that there is life elsewhere in the universe is plausible but not certain. We just do not know; there is not sufficient evidence to settle the question. The opinion that it is more important to study history than biology may be true; there is something to be said on both sides. That New Hampshire is a better place to live than Vermont is based mostly on preference. The claim that chocolate ice cream is better than vanilla is merely a matter of taste.

---

reality that may or may not be true; the same for all thinkers.

"What is in question is a kind of book reviewing which seems to be more and more popular: the loose putting down of opinions as though they were facts, and the treating of facts as though they were opinions."

Gore Vidal
New York Times, 5 July 1964

ASK YOURSELF:
Is my judgment one that I think is true, but am not certain? Do I expect that some others could legitimately disagree with it? If so, it is an opinion.

Virtue

Real goodness of character

Virtue is the consistent tendency to will and to do *good. It includes clarity of purpose and the ability to act in accord with that purpose. To be virtuous is to mean to do good, to say what we mean, and to do what we say.

If I am virtuous, I have an equal concern for myself and for others. I understand that such goods as life, *knowledge, *friendship, and beauty are intrinsically good: they are good in themselves, not just as means to something else. Such goods should be protected and promoted for all people. There is no reason for me to think that you desire or deserve these goods any less than I do. To be virtuous is to honor these goods wherever they come into play, in my life, in your life, and in the lives of others.

To be virtuous is to be honest even when presented with the opportunity to cheat and get away with it. If I am virtuous, I do not even consider copying the answers from someone else's exam. If I am given too much change at Wal-Mart, I go back to the register and return it. I stand by the wrongly accused person even when doing so will cost me, in time, money, or reputation. If I am virtuous, I am thoughtful in words and careful in actions. I do not knowingly promise more than I can deliver or intend to deliver.

Virtue is the firm desire always to do the pretense of goodness for the

ASK YOURSELF:
*Is my motive for acting
a genuine concern that
good should be done?
Am I equally concerned
for myself and others? If
so, my action is based on
virtue, not on hypocrisy.*

*"Virtue perfects both the doer
and the deed. Complete
virtue makes a person
good all around."*

Thomas Aquinas
On the Cardinal Virtues, Q. 2

Hypocrisy

Fake goodness of character

Hypocrisy is pretending to be good in order to get something we want. It includes deception and a willingness to manipulate others. The hypocrite does not mean what he says, nor do his actions follow his words.

If I am hypocritical, I pretend to have an equal concern for myself and others. I pretend to be concerned for intrinsic goods such as life, *knowledge, *friendship, and beauty. In reality, however, I am concerned for others only to the extent that I will benefit, and I look on all goods simply as means to my own *pleasure. We all fall short of our *moral ideals, which is lamentable. But our inability to live up to ideals we really hold is weakness, not hypocrisy.

If I pretend to be good so as to win the reputation for *virtue, I am a hypocrite. I might pretend to be your best friend, proclaiming my devotion to your happiness when all I really want is to use you to get to meet your friend or your sister. I am hypocritical if I talk a lot about the importance of *honesty but take advantage of someone's mistake to come out ahead in some monetary transaction. As a hypocrite, I make promises with apparently deep sincerity, all the while never really intending to fulfill what I promise.

---

good for its own sake; hypocrisy is
ake of personal advantage.

"No type of injustice is more glaring than that of the hypocrite who, in the very instant of being most false, makes the pretense of appearing virtuous."

Cicero
On Moral Obligation, Bk. 1, ch. 13

ASK YOURSELF:
Is my motive for acting a desire merely to appear good for the sake of gain or pleasure? Am I saying one thing while intending to do another? If so, I am guilty of hypocrisy.

Wisdom

Knowing what is good and how to achieve it

Wisdom is intelligence guided by *virtue. It is keen insight and *logical ability applied to the big picture — the ultimate meaning of life. The wise person knows what really is *good and how to live in harmony with it.

Not only does the wise person know how to order his own life in accordance with what is really good; he also cares about the *community and knows how to order and enrich the lives of others. If I am wise, I am concerned that we all become good, and I know how to make this ideal a reality. I insist on *virtues such as *justice and kindness, and I know how to nurture them in my own life and in the lives of those in my community. The wise person directs himself and others toward real *happiness.

Wisdom is something we gain through loving what is good and through hard work. It requires *maturity and experience. A good parent is wise. She knows what is important for human beings; she is concerned to pass this *knowledge on to her children; and she understands how to get her children to adopt what is true and good in their lives. A *leader, civic or religious, who directs the community in ways that allow individual and cooperative activities to flourish, is wise.

Both the clever and the wise are intelligent; but by desire, the intelligence of the wise

ASK YOURSELF:
Is this intelligence in the service of goodness? Does it help me and others by providing moral guidance? If so, it is wisdom.

"Prudence becomes wisdom when all conduct is controlled by the proper end of human living."

Thomas Aquinas
Summa Theologica, I, Q. 1, art. 6

Cleverness

Knowing how to achieve what we want

Cleverness is intelligence without a *moral direction. It is keen insight and *logical ability applied to whatever is desired. The clever person knows how to get things done, but is not necessarily concerned about what is really *good.

Not only may the clever person be ignorant of what is really good for himself; he may also be indifferent to the flourishing of the *community. If I am clever, I am an expert at achieving goals, but these goals need not be what is really best for me and for others. I do not especially care about the *virtues of *justice or kindness. It is not that I am bad, just that I am not particularly concerned with knowing what is truly good, nor with ordering my life so as to obtain real *happiness for myself and others.

Cleverness is a natural gift. Since it does not require experience, it shows up at all stages of life. A three-year-old can be an expert at getting her mother and father to do whatever she wants. A teenager may possess the technical expertise to write complicated computer programs. A *politician may excel at getting people to believe him even when he is clearly wrong. Although such intelligence is impressive, it is not wisdom, for it lacks a *mature, moral center.

---

whereas the intelligence of the clever is directed
is guided by justice and compassion.

"Knowledge that is divorced from justice should be called cunning rather than wisdom."

Cicero
On Moral Obligation, Bk. 1, ch. 19

ASK YOURSELF:
Is this raw intelligence? Does it help me get what I want but offer no moral guidance? If so, it is cleverness.

Wonder

Uncertainty that awakens the intellect

We wonder at things that we do not know but that we think are knowable. Wonder is the beginning of *knowledge. It calls on our intelligence. Without wonder, we could not learn.

We love to wonder. Wonder is a key feature of our humanity. Through it we reach beyond our current understanding of the world and our place in it, marveling at the hidden depths of nature and human nature. When I wonder, I am charmed by an intelligibility that I cannot fully grasp. Although I cannot master the object of wonder, I do not feel frustrated, but somehow elevated above my normal state of understanding. I seek the wonderful, trying to understand its cause.

We wonder at all sorts of things. We wonder at the things of nature — the beauty of a flower and the grace of a galloping horse. We wonder at the mathematical truth that there is no proportion between the circumference of a circle and its radius (no exact number for *pi*). We wonder at the distance to the stars. We wonder that we can understand, that we can *choose, that we can love. How is it that material beings such as ourselves can do these things? We wonder that we exist at all. We wonder at the beauty of artistic creations. We wonder at the generosity of *friends.

Although both wonder and bewilderment
some answer, while bewilderment

ASK YOURSELF:
*Am I full of
questions? Do
these questions
enliven my
interest? If so,
I am full of
wonder.*

*"Wonder is the feeling
of the philosopher, and
philosophy begins in wonder."*

Plato
Theaetetus 155d

Bewilderment

Uncertainty that frustrates the intellect

We are bewildered by things we do not know and cannot see how we could know. Bewilderment prevents *knowledge. It ties up the intelligence. In itself, bewilderment makes learning impossible.

We hate to be bewildered. Bewilderment frustrates the fulfillment of our humanity, for it prevents *reason from succeeding in understanding the world and our place in it. When I am bewildered, I am paralyzed by the inability to sort out conflicting *evidence or ideas. I am disoriented, lost in a kind of darkness. Since I cannot understand, I cannot choose meaningfully. There is nothing elevating about being confused. I flee bewilderment and seek to eliminate its cause.

We are bewildered when our desire for knowledge is frustrated either because our sense experiences are distorted in some way or because our ideas are unclear or confusing. We are bewildered when we have to find our way in the pitch black of night or the white-out of a heavy snowstorm. We are bewildered when what we thought was true now appears to be false, or vice versa. *Moral confusion is also bewildering: how can we choose between two things if we do not have any way of knowing which one is preferable? We are bewildered when we do not know whom to trust.

---

involve uncertainty, wonder promises
offers no hope of understanding.

≋

"Men at first had eyes but saw to no purpose; they had ears but did not hear. Like the shapes of dreams they dragged through their long lives and handled all things in bewilderment and confusion."

Aeschylus
Prometheus Bound, 445

ASK YOURSELF:
Am I full of questions?
Do these questions confuse me?
If so, I am bewildered.

For further reading and reflection

Admiration/Envy

On how envy distorts the appreciation of good that is admiration, see Dante's *Divine Comedy*, "Purgatory," Cantos 13 and 14. For a more systematic and technical account of envy, see Thomas Aquinas, *On Evil*, Question 10. For a contemporary treatment of envy, see Henry Fairlie, *The Seven Deadly Sins Today*, a secular account of how pride, envy, anger, sloth, avarice, gluttony, and lust affect us today.

Authority/Power

On the nature of true authority, see Plato's discussion in *The Statesman* (in particular, 292b-294a). Here he makes an analogy between what constitutes authority in government and what constitutes authority in medicine. For Plato, authority is the prerequisite for exercising power. On the claim that power is the ultimate source of all authority, see Thomas Hobbes's *Leviathan*, especially Part I, Chapters 15 and 16.

Certainty/Inflexibility

On certainty, see Aristotle's discussion of the most basic and certain principle on which all reality and thought depend. This is discussed in his *Metaphysics*, Book 4, Chapter 3. See also Augustine's discussion of the limits of doubt in *City of God*, Book 11, Chapter 26.

On inflexibility, see the example of Thrasymachus in Plato's *Republic*, Book 1. Thrasymachus absolutely refuses to agree with Socrates, even when he sees that what Socrates says is true.

Character/Personality

On character, see Plato's account, in his dialogues *Apology* and *Crito*, of the great example, in word and deed, of Socrates. Although Socrates has an interesting personality, it is his character that is most impressive. See also the example of Thomas More in Robert Bolt's *A Man for All Seasons* (play and movie).

Chastity/Prudery

On the virtue of chastity, see the discussion by Thomas Aquinas in his *Summa Theologica*, II-II, Question 151, where he speaks of chastity as the moderation of the desire for sexual gratification. Like all virtues, this moderation is guided by reason. Since reason recognizes that sexual desire is natural and that the fruit of sexual union is good, the extreme of avoiding any reference to sexuality (prudery) is to be avoided.

Choice/Impulse

On what constitutes choice and its responsibilities, see Aristotle's discussion on the voluntary in the first half of Book 3 in his *Nicomachean Ethics*. See also Augustine's excellent work *On Free Choice of the Will*. On the point that we should always act from reasoned choice and not impulse, see Cicero, *On Moral Obligation*, Book 1, Chapters 28-30.

Citizen/Resident

On being a good citizen, see Aristotle's *Politics*, Book 3, Chapters 1-4. Key to Aristotle's notion here is that a citizen is committed to preserving the common good under a particular constitution and also knows how to rule and be ruled. See also *The Federalist Papers*, where the Founding Fathers of the United States discuss the rights and responsibilities of being a good citizen.

Commitment/Fanaticism

On the importance of commitment but the unreasonableness of fanaticism, see the discussion by John Finnis about the twin requirements of detachment and commitment in Chapter 5 of his *Natural Law and Natural Rights*. Our pursuit of human flourishing cannot succeed unless we persevere; this requires commitment. On the other hand, since there are a variety of fundamental human goods worth pursuing, it is unreasonable to focus exclusively on one, especially when this means violating another.

Community/Group

On community, see Aristotle's discussion, in his *Politics*, Book 1, Chapter 2, of the naturalness of human beings living in a community and his assertion that a community is more than just a group (*Politics*, Book 3, Chapter 9). See also Cicero's discussion of justice and communities in *On Moral Obligation*, Book 1, Chapters 7-10 and 15-17.

Confidence/Pride

On the importance and goodness of confidence, see Aristotle, *Nicomachean Ethics,* Book 4, Chapter 3. Aristotle speaks of what is sometimes translated as "proper pride," which is the appropriate confidence in our own ability.

On the sin of pride, see Dante's *Divine Comedy,* "Purgatory," Cantos 10-13. For a more systematic and technical account of pride, see Thomas Aquinas, *On Evil,* Question 8. For a contemporary treatment of pride, see Henry Fairlie, *The Seven Deadly Sins Today,* a secular account of how pride, envy, anger, sloth, avarice, gluttony, and lust affect us today.

Conscience/Feelings

On conscience, see the important distinctions made by Thomas Aquinas in his *Summa Theologica,* I-II, Question 19, articles 5 and 6. Aquinas's basic point is that we should always follow an informed conscience. For the notion that it is feeling or a kind of moral sense that guides us, see David Hume's discussion in *An Enquiry Concerning the Principles of Morals,* Section 9.

Courage/Rashness

On the virtue of courage and how it differs from rashness, see Aristotle, *Nicomachean Ethics,* Book 3, Chapters 6-9. As with all the virtues, it is reason that sees the difference between acting courageously and being foolish. Cicero gives a somewhat more general account in *On Moral Obligation,* Book 1, Chapters 19-26. See also the discussion of fortitude by Josef Pieper in *The Four Cardinal Virtues.*

Creativity/Skillfulness

On creativity, see Aristotle's short work *Poetics,* in which he speaks about what makes a good work of literary art. See also Thomas Aquinas's discussion of art in *Summa Theologica,* I-II, Question 57, articles 3 and 4. Immanuel Kant discusses the relation between genius and taste in producing art in his *Critique of Judgment,* Part 1, Division 1, Book 2, paragraphs 48-50. Here he concludes that creating fine art requires imagination, understanding, spirit, and taste.

Criticism/Condemnation

On what constitutes the proper grounds and procedure for criticism, see C. S. Lewis, *The Abolition of Man,* Chapter 2 (last third). Proper criticism is not the rejection of another person or even of all that the person holds to be true or worthwhile. Rather, it is a careful pointing out that someone's idea or value is inconsistent with some other more basic idea or value that the person holds as certain.

Dependency/Subjugation
On the naturalness and goodness of interdependence in the human community, see Plato's *Republic,* especially Book 4, where he discusses the importance of having people work together, depending on each other for the good of the community. On the wrongfulness of subjugation, see Abraham Lincoln's work denouncing slavery: *Fragment on Slavery.*

Discussion/Argument
For examples of discussion, see the dialogues of Plato, in particular the *Euthyphro* and *The Republic,* Book 1, where the ideal is for each party to say honestly what he thinks is true and to yield to the truth when it becomes clear. The dialogues of Augustine are examples of the same procedure. See, in particular, *On Free Choice of the Will.*

Error/Fault
On the necessity of deliberation and free choice for there to be fault, see Aristotle's discussion of the voluntary in *Nicomachean Ethics,* Book 3, Chapters 1-5. As Aristotle says, in *Nicomachean Ethics,* Book 2, Chapter 3, for an act to be praiseworthy or blameworthy, it must be done with knowledge and intentionally, not by mistake or unintentionally.

Evidence/Intuition
On the need for evidence in the sciences, see Francis Bacon, *The New Organon,* Author's Preface. This need is implicit in the scientific method: hypothesis and verification. An idea is one thing, but we need experimental evidence that the idea is true. Evidence is also required in other areas of thought, such as mathematics and ethics. To prove anything, we need evidence of some kind that is accessible to us all.

Excellence/Popularity
On the distinction between excellence and popularity, see Plato's claim in the *Crito* that we should always do what is really good, not just what the majority is doing or would do. See also Aristotle's point, which he makes in his *Rhetoric,* Book 1, Chapter 1, about the importance of using the art of persuasion (which appeals to what is popular with an audience) to support what is truly good.

Fairness/Equality
For a discussion of the difference between fairness and equality, see Aristotle's discussion of distributive justice in Book 5 of his *Nicomachean Ethics.* Here he says that there must be a proportion between what is deserved and what is given: a well-deserving person should not be shortchanged, nor a less-deserving person overcompensated. To give both parties an equal share would be unfair.

Faith/Gullibility
On the difference between faith and gullibility, see C. S. Lewis's essay, "On Obstinacy in Belief." In the essay, Lewis argues that certain kinds of beliefs are reasonable and even necessary for us to lead intelligent and moral lives. As W. K. Clifford points out in his essay "The Ethics of Belief," to believe beyond all evidence (to be gullible) is not a virtue.

Fidelity/Idolatry
On the importance of fidelity or loyalty in our lives, see Gabriel Marcel's discussion of creative fidelity in his essay "On the Ontological Mystery" in his book *The Philosophy of Existentialism.* Marcel speaks of keeping ourselves open to the world and others, of being ready and willing to commit ourselves to discovering truth and nurturing goodness. See also Josiah Royce's book *The Philosophy of Loyalty* (in particular, Lecture 1). In this work, Royce speaks of the necessity of loyalty for human relations, but also recognizes its limits and the dangers of idolatry.

Forgiveness/Pardon
On forgiveness, see the account of the virtues needed to live a good life given by the Stoic philosopher Marcus Aurelius in the first book of his *Meditations.* He commends several times the willingness to put aside hard feelings and renew friendly relations with those who have caused us harm. To hate others is in some way to harm ourselves. See also Sophocles's play *Antigone.* At the center of the play, Antigone counsels Creon to give up hatred and embrace the reconciliation of love.

Frankness/Rudeness
On frankness, see the discussion in Plato's *Republic,* Book 2, where even those who agree with Socrates (Glaucon and Adeimantus) press the opposite position with candor. For an example of a person who speaks with frankness on all manner of subjects, see the conversations of Samuel Johnson as recorded by his friend James Boswell in his *Life of Johnson.*

Freedom/License
On the idea of a freedom that is compatible with the responsibilities of living in a community, see the *Declaration of Independence.* We have a right to liberty, but not to license: the ideal of democratic equality forbids the anarchy of doing whatever we feel like doing. For more on the difference between moral freedom and license (freedom to do as we please), see the first chapter of *Beyond the New Morality,* by Germain Grisez and Russell Shaw.

Friendship/Fellowship
Out of the ten books of his *Nicomachean Ethics,* Aristotle devotes two (Books 8 and 9) to friendship. This is a wonderful resource for important distinctions between friendship in the full sense and relationships that are somewhat like it, such as useful or pleasant acquaintances. See also Cicero's work *On Friendship.*

Genius/Eccentricity
On artistic genius, see Immanuel Kant's discussion in his *Critique of Judgment,* Part 1, Division 1, Book 2, paragraphs 46-50. Here Kant limits genius to art, not science; but it seems that, just as genius gives a rule to art and provides a kind of new standard, so genius in intellectual pursuits may do the same, bringing new vision to our way of understanding reality.

Goodness/Usefulness
On the distinction between goodness and usefulness, see Aristotle's discussion in his *Nicomachean Ethics,* Book 8, Chapters 2-5. Aristotle distinguishes three reasons why something may be desired: it is useful, pleasant, or good. Kant makes essentially the same point in his *Fundamental Principles of the Metaphysics of Morals,* First Section, when he talks about the three motives we may have for doing something: self-interest (usefulness), direct inclination (pleasure), and duty (because it is a good thing to do).

Gratitude/Indebtedness
On gratitude, see Aristotle's discussion in his *Nicomachean Ethics,* Book 8, Chapter 16 through Book 9, Chapter 2. When we are unable to repay someone in kind for some good we have received, gratitude is appropriate. This is true for our relations to parents (who have given us life), to teachers (who have opened the way to truth for us), and to the source of all being, whom we call God (who has given us everything).

Greatness/Fame
On true greatness and nobility, see Cicero's *On Moral Obligation,* Book 1, where Cicero says that the fulfillment of our human nature, true greatness, is accomplished by being wise, just, courageous, and moderate. On the limited goodness of fame, see Boethius's *Consolation of Philosophy,* Book 2, Prose 7 and Poem 7, and Book 3, Prose 6 and Poem 6. Here Boethius argues that happiness cannot be found in fame, since it is fleeting and depends on other people.

Happiness/Pleasure

On the distinction between happiness and pleasure, see Aristotle's discussion in his *Nicomachean Ethics,* Books 1 and 10. Although pleasure is an element in happiness, it is far less essential than wisdom or virtue. See also Boethius's consideration of what constitutes real happiness in Book 3 of his *Consolation of Philosophy.*

Honesty/Naïveté

On the nobility of honesty, see the example of Socrates in Plato's *Apology.* Socrates prefers to stick to what is true and good, even though doing so is not in his self-interest. Also, on the importance of honesty for community, see Immanuel Kant's *Fundamental Principles of the Metaphysics of Morals,* First and Second Sections. Kant says that we have a perfect duty to tell the truth. Without honesty, human society is impossible.

Honor/Flattery

On the difference between true honor, which is based on virtue, and the public acclaim that may be mere flattery, see Boethius, *The Consolation of Philosophy,* Book 3. See also the speech by Don Quixote in the beginning of Chapter 32 of *Don Quixote* by Miguel de Cervantes, where he renounces flattery but professes a desire to attain true honor.

Hope/Wish

On the meaning of hope and the importance of it in our lives, see Gabriel Marcel's essay "On the Ontological Mystery" in his book *The Philosophy of Existentialism.* Here Marcel speaks of hope as an active expectation of the good things that are possible and a willingness to participate in bringing them to fruition, rather than as a passive wish.

Humility/Self-contempt

On what constitutes proper humility, as opposed to self-contempt, see Aristotle's discussion of this virtue in *Nicomachean Ethics,* Book 4, Chapter 3. Humility is, above all, truthful. To denigrate ourselves beyond what is true is therefore wrong. This is especially harmful, for if we do not think we have any real value or talent, we will not demand anything of ourselves. See also the discussion of humility by Thomas Aquinas in his *Summa Theologica,* II-II, Question 161, articles 1, 4, and 5.

Impartiality/Indifference

On the importance of impartiality, see Immanuel Kant, *Fundamental Principles of the Metaphysics of Morals,* Second Section. Kant proposes as a central moral principle that we should always treat human beings, ourselves and others, as ends (of ultimate importance) and never merely as means to ends (as useful tools). This obviously rules out indifference, and it demands impartiality. See also John Finnis's emphasis on this point in his *Natural Law and Natural Rights*, Chapter 5.

Importance/Excitement

On importance as a category of meaning and value, see Plato on the proper order of the parts of the soul in *The Republic,* Book 4. Plato holds that there are three parts of the soul: the rational part, the spirited or emotional part, and the appetitive or sensual part. Excitement appeals to the emotional and sensual parts, importance to the rational part. Plato holds that we can be happy only if our souls are ordered. Since putting things in order is an activity of reason, the rational part must make decisions about the relative importance of things.

Individualism/Egoism

On the importance of every individual, see Immanuel Kant, *Fundamental Principles of the Metaphysics of Morals,* Second Section. Here Kant insists that every human being be treated as a person with dignity and autonomy, and never as a thing to be used to promote some sweeping political or social agenda. Every person counts, and every person has a responsibility to the community.

On egoism as the foundation for morality and government, see Thomas Hobbes's *Leviathan,* especially Chapter 13, where he speaks of the naturally selfish condition of human beings, and Chapters 14 and 15, where he attempts to show that constant attention to this self-interest will lead to compromise and a stable government.

Joy/Exuberance

On joy as distinct from exuberance or delight, see Thomas Aquinas's discussion in his *Summa Theologica,* I-II, Question 31, article 3. Here Aquinas points out that joy always has an element of reason in it, whereas delight may be the satisfaction or stimulation of sensual or emotional desires. See also John Locke's discussion of joy in his *Essay Concerning Human Understanding,* Book 2, Chapter 20. Locke stresses that joy is found in the mind's consideration or expectation of something good.

Judgment/Prejudice

On judgment, see Boethius's *Consolation of Philosophy,* Books 1 and 2, where Lady Philosophy challenges a perturbed Boethius to think clearly about what is true and what is good.

On prejudice, see Lincoln's letter in which he rejects prejudice against blacks, foreigners, and Catholics (Abraham Lincoln, Letter to Joshua F. Sheed, 24 August 1855). See also the inspiring speech "I Have a Dream," by Martin Luther King, Jr., on the wrongfulness of judging people by the color of their skin.

Justice/Law

On justice, see Plato's great work, *The Republic.* "What is justice?" is the question that informs the entire work. See Aristotle's discussion of justice in Book 5 of his *Nicomachean Ethics* and Cicero's in his work *On Moral Obligation*, Book 1, Chapters 7-18.

On the relation between justice and law, Thomas Aquinas says that only laws that are just are real laws. See his *Summa Theologica,* I-II, Question 95, articles 1 and 2. Thomas Hobbes, on the other hand, thinks that justice is what the laws say it is, and the laws are made by whoever has the power to enforce them. See his *Leviathan,* Part I, Chapters 15-18.

Knowledge/Information

On our natural love for knowledge and the process by which we come to know, see Aristotle's discussion in his *Metaphysics,* Book 1, Chapters 1 and 2. See also the detailed account given by Thomas Aquinas in his *Summa Theologica,* I, Question 84, especially articles 1 and 6. Here Aquinas speaks about how we are able to learn from the material things we experience. From the images we receive through the senses (raw information), we come to know the natures of things.

Leader/Trendsetter

On the difference between leading and being popular, see the discussion by Plato on the real purpose of leading or ruling in Book 1 of his *Republic.* See also his discussion in Book 6, where he distinguishes between the sophist who appeals to the preferences of the crowd to gain and retain popularity and the philosophical leader who pursues what is true and good and who tries to communicate this to his followers.

Love/Lust

On the distinction between love and lust, see John Milton's *Paradise Lost:* on love, Book 4, lines 610-775; on lust, Book 9, lines 1013-1131. See also Shakespeare's Sonnets 116 (on love) and 129 (on lust). A good discussion of the distinction is to be found in Henry Fairlie's *The Seven Deadly Sins Today,* in which Fairlie discusses pride, envy, anger, sloth, avarice, gluttony, and lust in terms of how they can be found in our lives, whether or not we believe in God or the theology of sin.

Maturity/Adulthood
On what constitutes maturity, see Plato's discussion, near the end of his *Republic*, Book 7, concerning the stages of education. According to Plato, full maturity and readiness to rule would be achieved only around age fifty. However, the main point is not the age, for there are many foolish people who are fifty or older; rather, it is the domination of reason over passion. Aristotle makes a similar point in his *Nicomachean Ethics*, Book 1, Chapter 1, when he says that immature people (not just in years but in attitude) do not make good students of ethics. This is because they are led by passions and not by reason.

Mercy/Laxness
On the distinction between mercy and laxness, see C. S. Lewis's essay "The Humanitarian Theory of Punishment." Lewis argues that mercy detached from justice is actually unmerciful. In other words, mercy is an ally of justice, to be granted when it is reasonable to do so for the good of the person to be punished and for the good of the community.

Morality/Custom
On the difference between morality and custom, see Sophocles's play *Antigone*, where the tension between the law of the state and some deeper natural law is presented. See also Plato's *Apology*, where Socrates is condemned according to legal due process for acting in ways that support morality, and see his *Crito*, where Socrates argues for an ethics based on reason, not just on feeling or majority opinion. In his book *The Abolition of Man*, C. S. Lewis presents the case for moral principles transcending culture. See, in particular, Chapter 2 and the Appendix.

Mystery/Problem
On the difference between mystery and problem, see Gabriel Marcel's essay "On the Ontological Mystery" in his book *The Philosophy of Existentialism*. Whereas a problem is the kind of thing that can and therefore should be solved, a mystery is something that does not admit of final categorical solution. See also Frank Sheed's discussion of mystery in *Theology and Sanity*, Chapter 2, and G. K. Chesterton's treatment of the matter at the end of the second chapter of his book *Orthodoxy*.

Norm/Average
On the distinction between what is a standard and what most people think or do, see Plato's *Crito.* Here Crito tries to get Socrates to think and do what the average person would, but Socrates insists on doing what is right, even if only one person is doing it. Cicero makes the same point in his work *On Moral Obligation,* Book 1, Chapter 3, where he says that such things as life, knowledge, and friendship are goods that should be honored even if no one, in fact, honors them.

Obedience/Servility
On obedience, see Plato's *Crito,* where Socrates emphasizes the importance of being obedient to reason, but also to the laws of the state. This does not mean blind servility, for he allows that it is permissible to try to convince the state that the laws are wrong. See also the fine example found in *The Rule of Saint Benedict.* Benedict, in setting forth the rules for living in a monastic community, stresses the importance of obedience as the willingness to listen and to follow what is best, not just for ourselves, but for the whole community.

Open-mindedness/Indiscrimination
On the critical distinction between being open-minded and failing to discriminate, see C. S. Lewis's *The Abolition of Man,* especially Chapter 2. Here Lewis says that it is good to be open-minded, to listen to all rational arguments and to consider all evidence. However, this open-mindedness should not extend to the possibility that there might not be any truth or that there might not be any value in trying to be good. To think that there is no truth or that no action is better than any other is not to be open-minded, but to abandon any attempt at rational discrimination. It is to shut down reason, rather than to pursue free inquiry. See also G. K. Chesterton's *Orthodoxy,* Chapter 3: "The Suicide of Thought."

Pain/Evil
On the difference between pain and moral evil, see the discussion by Thomas Aquinas in his *Summa Theologica,* I, Question 48, articles 5 and 6. For a more contemporary discussion of the distinction, see Herbert McCabe's discussion in "Evil" in his book *God Matters.*

Patience/Passivity
On patience, see Augustine's work *On Patience* and also Thomas Aquinas's treatment of the issue in his *Summa Theologica,* II-II, Question 136. Here Aquinas emphasizes the necessity of patience

to help us face pain and sorrow so they do not deflect us from our commitment to following what reason tells us is true and good.

Patriotism/Nationalism
On the obligation to love and honor our country, see Plato in his *Crito,* where he draws an analogy between obligations to parents and obligations to country. Cicero makes the same point in his work *On Moral Obligation,* Book 1, Chapter 17.

On the dangers of fanatical nationalism, see G. K. Chesterton's *The End of the Armistice,* in which he criticizes the nationalism of the Nazis.

Peace/Truce
On peace and how it differs from mere cessation of fighting, see Augustine's discussion in *City of God,* Book 9, Chapters 11-14, about how peace is a principle of nature as well as of personal moral fitness and community life. See also the discussion of peace by Thomas Aquinas in his *Summa Theologica,* II-II, Question 29. Abraham Lincoln's *Second Inaugural Address* also expresses well the nature of peace.

Politeness/Phoniness
On the importance of being polite, see Jane Austen's novels, especially *Emma.* The contrast between the excellent manners of Knightly and the frequent rudeness of Emma (up until the end) is striking. Courtesy, although not perhaps full-blown virtue, is a close relative, for the effort to be courteous indicates a virtuous choice to promote community.

For an example of false courtesy or phoniness, consider the sister of Mr. Bingley in Austen's *Pride and Prejudice* or, indeed, the great Catherine De Bourgh herself (Darcy's aunt). (There are also excellent videos available portraying both these novels.)

Politics/Partisanship
On the nobility of political activity and its distinction from partisanship, see Plato's *Republic,* Book 1, where Socrates insists that the true political ruler is concerned for the good of those who are ruled. See also the end of Aristotle's *Nicomachean Ethics,* where he emphasizes the practical nature of ethics. It is one thing to know how we should live: it is another thing — and a noble calling — to take the actions that make these ideals a reality in the community. For examples of leaders who have shown (and, in some cases, failed to show) this political spirit, see Plutarch's *Lives* of the great figures of Greek and Roman politics.

Profundity/Obscurity
On profundity in literature, see Aristotle's *Poetics,* in which he focuses especially on tragedy and on the importance of plot in a tragedy's success. Sophocles's *Oedipus Rex* moves us deeply because of the well-orchestrated turnings of the plot, which surprise us and evoke deep psychological feelings of pity, fear, and wonder. Likewise, the ultimate conclusions of metaphysics are profound: as Thomas Aquinas says in his *Summa Theologica,* I, Preface to Question 3, although we can know that a first cause of all things exists, we cannot know what it is (its essence), but only what it is not. Obscurity creeps into tragedy when the plot is unclear or without plausibility and into philosophy when the terminology is inconsistent or the ideas incoherent.

Progress/Change
On the idea of progress in science and technology, see Francis Bacon's Preface to *The Great Instauration.* Alfred North Whitehead comments on the success of the scientific method in the first chapter of his book *Science and the Modern World.* On the distinction between real progress and mere change, see G. K. Chesterton's discussion of "the false theory of progress" in *Orthodoxy,* Chapter 3: "The Suicide of Thought." C. S. Lewis touches upon the same theme in *The Abolition of Man.* In Chapter 2 he denies the possibility of innovating radically new values, and in Chapter 3 he warns that, in some of its aspects at least, progress in science and technology could be a threat to the moral well-being of humanity.

Proof/Persuasion
On the important distinction between proof and persuasion, see Plato's *Apology.* At the beginning, Socrates notes how persuasive his accuser was in his speech, but also how false the accusations were. Socrates goes on to disprove his accusers' charges and to prove in word and in deed his innocence of the charges. See also Aristotle's *Rhetoric.* This book focuses on the best ways to convince an audience. Aristotle holds that persuasion ought to be used to promote what is true and good. However, he also understands that its methods are not the same as those of strict logical proof.

Prosperity/Wealth
On the difference between prosperity as a kind of fullness of flourishing and the possession of wealth, see Aristotle's *Nicomachean Ethics,* Books 1 and 10. The ability to get material possessions and the pleasures they bring are aspects of prospering, but they are not the most

important parts: wisdom and virtue are much more fundamental.
See also Boethius's discussion of the limited goodness of wealth in
his *Consolation of Philosophy,* Books 2 and 3.

Prudence/Cowardice
On the virtue of prudence, see Aristotle's *Nicomachean Ethics,* Book 7.
Prudence is the ability to make choices that bring about good states of
affairs and good institutions in the world. Such choices often require a
certain caution, since a frontal attack on vice and wrongdoers may end
up failing to bring about the good it intends. However, such caution is
not cowardice, but a matter of wise choice. See also Josef Pieper's discussion of prudence in *The Four Cardinal Virtues.*

Punishment/Revenge
On the distinction between punishment and revenge, see C. S. Lewis's
essay "The Humanitarian Theory of Punishment." Here he argues for
making fairness — what is best for the community and the criminal —
the prime factor in punishment. In his *Summa Theologica,* II-II, Question
64, article 7, on killing in self-defense, Thomas Aquinas argues that
the direct intention to harm another, even to pay back an injustice, is
never justified. See also Immanuel Kant's discussion of revenge in his
Lectures on Ethics, "Vengeance."

Questioning/Skepticism
On the importance of questioning, see the great example of Socrates
in Plato's dialogues. Socrates pursues the truth by a relentless series
of questions. In his *Apology,* he makes the famous statement that the
unexamined life is not worth living. And in Book 1 of *The Republic,*
he continually encourages Thrasymachus (with whom he disagrees)
not to admit something that he does not really believe. On the disaster
that occurs when questioning passes over into skepticism, see G. K.
Chesterton's discussion in *Orthodoxy,* Chapter 3: "The Suicide of
Thought."

Reality/Matter
On reality that transcends the limits of materiality, see Plato's discussion of the levels of reality in *The Republic* at the end of Book 6,
where he presents "the divided line," and at the beginning of Book 7,
where he presents, as an explanatory story, "the analogy of the cave."
See also Thomas Aquinas's discussions in his *Summa Theologica,* I,
Question 75, articles 2-6 and Question 83, article 4, where he says
that the rational soul and freedom of choice are not bound by the
limitations of matter.

Reason/Logic
On logic as the art of demonstration, see Aristotle's *Prior Analytics,* Book 1, Chapter 1. Logic is the way we reason correctly, but it has no content of its own. Reason, on the other hand, is concerned with three distinct objects: truth, goodness, and beauty. On the distinction between theoretical reason (whose object is truth) and practical reason (whose object is goodness), see Thomas Aquinas, *Summa Theologica,* I-II, Question 94, article 2. On reason as it apprehends beauty, see Aristotle's *Poetics.*

Reform/Rebellion
On the distinction between reform and rebellion, see the discussion by C. S. Lewis in his *Abolition of Man,* Chapter 2. Lewis argues that legitimate reform in ethics or politics builds on the ideals recognized by the party or institution that needs reform. Thus, in reform, there is continuity between a past state of affairs (the recognition of an ideal) and a future aim (the realization of that ideal). Rebellion, on the other hand, destroys this continuity, abandoning past ideals or institutions in favor of new ones. G. K. Chesterton makes the same point in *Orthodoxy,* Chapter 7: "The Eternal Revolution."

Respect/Fear
On the nature of respect, see Immanuel Kant's discussion in his *Fundamental Principles of the Metaphysics of Morals,* First Section, especially footnote 3. Here Kant says that we respect people who stand for what we ourselves know to be right; thus, respect is ultimately grounded in our recognition of the universal moral law. On fear as a motivator, see Niccolo Machiavelli's *The Prince,* Chapter 17. Here he says that it is better for a ruler to be feared than to be loved, because it is in his power to instill fear but not to elicit love and respect.

Responsibility/Restriction
On the distinction between responsibility and restriction, see Immanuel Kant's discussion of the nature of duty in his *Fundamental Principles of the Metaphysics of Morals,* First and Second Sections. Kant says that the demands of morality are not arbitrary restrictions imposed upon us; they are the demands of our own reason, which has direct insight into the universal and unchanging principles of moral obligation. See also the discussion of freedom, responsibility, and self-determination by Germain Grisez and Russell Shaw in *Beyond the New Morality,* Chapters 1 and 2.

Reverence/Superstition
On the importance of reverence for all aspects of our lives, see the discussion in Chapter 1 of *The Art of Living,* by Dietrich and Alice von

Hildebrand. All existence should be the object of reverence. On the dangers of superstition, see the discussion by Thomas Aquinas in his *Summa Theologica*, II-II, Question 92, articles 1 and 2. Here Aquinas insists that things should not be revered more than they are worth. Specifically, no creature should be honored as the creator.

Right/Want

On human rights, see the *Declaration of Independence* and *The Bill of Rights*. It is clear that the rights we are due are limited. For the distinction between rights and wants, see the discussion by Henry Fairlie in *The Seven Deadly Sins Today*, Chapter 3: "Anger." For a more extensive treatment of the relationship between moral obligation and rights, see John Finnis's book *Natural Law and Natural Rights*.

Ruler/Tyrant

On the difference between a ruler, who cares for the people, and a tyrant, who wants to have things his way, see Sophocles's *Antigone*. See also Plato's famous analogy comparing a ruler with a shepherd in *The Republic*, Book 1, 345c-345e. On the specific comparison between a ruler (king) and a tyrant, see Aristotle, *Nicomachean Ethics*, Book 8, Chapters 12 and 13 and *Politics*, Book 5, Chapter 10. On the same subject, see also Thomas Aquinas's *On Kingship*, Book 1, Chapters 1 and 6.

Self-control/Repression

On the virtue of self-control, or temperance, and how it is not the repression or extermination of desire, see Aristotle, *Nicomachean Ethics*, Book 3, Chapters 10-12. Cicero presents a good discussion of self-control in his work *On Moral Obligation*, Book 1, Chapters 27 and 28. See also the more contemporary discussion of temperance by Josef Pieper in *The Four Cardinal Virtues*.

Self-examination/Self-absorption

On self-examination, see the great example of Socrates as portrayed in Plato's *Apology*. Socrates is constantly asking himself what is the best way to live. For the contrast between self-examination and self-absorption, see the difference between Socrates and Euthyphro in Plato's dialogue *Euthyphro*. For a discussion of the dangers of failing to examine our lives and falling into self-absorption, see Henry Fairlie's book *The Seven Deadly Sins Today*.

Self-respect/Self-satisfaction

On the importance of self-respect, see Immanuel Kant's discussion of moral obligation in *Fundamental Principles of the Metaphysics* of Morals, Second Section. When formulating his ethical principle, Kant says that we should always treat human beings — ourselves and others — as an end and never merely as a means to an end. Every human being, including ourselves, must be respected. See also his essay "Proper Self-Respect." On the danger of self-satisfaction, see Plato's *Euthyphro* in which the character Euthyphro, because he thinks he has all the answers, cannot learn and rushes off to prosecute his father without knowing whether his action is just.

Simplicity/Foolishness
On noble simplicity, see the description of the just person that Glaucon presents at the beginning of Book 2 of Plato's *Republic*. Such a person does what is good for its own sake, disregarding any advantage or disadvantage that doing good might bring.

On foolishness, see the discussion of imprudence by Thomas Aquinas in his *Summa Theologica*, II-II, Question 53, article 1. To be imprudent or foolish is to expose ourselves to bad consequences without necessity.

Sophistication/Snobbishness
On sophistication, see John Henry Newman's discussion, in his *Idea of a University*, Discourses 5-7, of the person well educated in the liberal arts. Such a person is ready to enter into any social circle and to take up any kind of work. Sophistication turns to snobbishness when, just because a person has been to the finest schools or is part of high society, he looks down on others. On snobbishness, see the examples of Bingley's sister and Lady Catherine De Bourgh in Jane Austen's novel *Pride and Prejudice.*

Stability/Stagnation
On the necessity of stability for the growth of community, see the discussion in Book 2 of Plato's *Republic* on the beginnings of the city. Without stability, there can be no development of community from its rudimentary life-sustaining purposes to its fruition as a place for education in knowledge and virtue. As Socrates says in Plato's *Apology*, there is a danger that fixed customs and routines may cause the community to stagnate. We must continue to strive for knowledge and virtue. As Socrates says, "The unexamined life is not worth living."

Statesman/Demagogue
On the difference between a statesman and a demagogue, see Plato's discussion in *The Republic*, Book 6. Here he distinguishes

between the great speaker, who seeks popularity and power by appealing to the passions of the crowd, and the committed statesman, who pursues truth and virtue and tries to encourage a love for these in those he governs. See also Aristotle's discussions in his *Nicomachean Ethics*, Book 10, Chapter 10 and in his *Politics*, Book 7, Chapters 1-3. There he insists that the true statesman has a high moral character as well as the practical ability to guide others toward personal virtue and community.

Student/Disciple
On the essence of being a student, see Aristotle's *Metaphysics*, Book 1, Chapters 1 and 2. Here he says that we all naturally desire to know. This natural desire lives in the student, who is motivated by a deep desire to know what is true and good. See also the discussion by John Henry Newman in his *Idea of a University*, Discourse 5, where he insists that the student's intellectual world be as broad as possible and not limited by conformity to a particular kind of knowledge or the teaching of a particular person.

Tenacity/Stubbornness
On the distinction between tenacity and stubbornness, see Book 1 of Plato's *Republic*. In the central discussion between Socrates and Thrasymachus, Socrates insists that Thrasymachus should abandon his position only if he sees that it is wrong. He should not give in out of fear or a desire to be accepted. However, when Thrasymachus has twice come to admit that his position is wrong yet still refuses to abandon it, he is merely being stubborn.

Thinking/Imagining
On the difference between thinking and imagining, see Plato's discussion in his *Phaedo*, 74b-79d. When we pursue the meaning of such things as equality, justice, and beauty, we move from picturing particular examples to thinking about what they all have in common. See also Frank Sheed's discussion about the difference between thinking and imagining (what he calls "picture-thinking") in *Theology and Sanity*, Chapter 2. Unless we move from imagining to thinking, we cannot have knowledge.

Tolerance/Relativism
On the insight that grounds the virtue of tolerance, see Immanuel Kant's discussion of moral obligation in *Fundamental Principles of the Metaphysics of Morals*, Second Section. Kant says that every human being should always be treated as an end (that is, as having

ultimate value) and never merely as a means to an end. Every human being must be respected. Such a strong moral principle is obviously incompatible with relativism. On the insufficiency of relativism, see the discussion by Germain Grisez and Russell Shaw in *Beyond the New Morality*, Chapter 6.

Tradition/The Past
On tradition as something relevant to the present and not just a relic of the past, see G. K. Chesterton's discussion in *Orthodoxy*, Chapter 4: "The Ethics of Elfland." *Tradition* means being aware of and open to the great majority of people who have lived. See also Ralph McInerny's discussion of tradition in his book *Thomism in an Age of Renewal*, Chapter 2: "Tradition and Philosophy." Here he distinguishes between a living tradition that enriches our lives and the mere baggage of an uncritically accepted past, which weighs us down.

Truth/Opinion
On the difference between knowing the truth and having an opinion, see Plato's *Meno* 97a-98b. Even if the opinion is correct, it is not known to be correct. When something is known to be correct, the knower possesses the truth, which is the same for him and for others. See also Thomas Aquinas's discussion in his *Summa Theologica*, I, Question 16, article 1. Here Aquinas speaks of the essence of truth, which is the conformity of the intellect to the thing understood. Opinion may or may not be in conformity with the thing understood.

Virtue/Hypocrisy
On virtue, see Aristotle's *Nicomachean Ethics*, especially Books 2 and 3, on the kinds of moral virtue and how we can acquire them. There is a nice summary of the cardinal virtues (wisdom, justice, courage, and temperance) in Cicero's *On Moral Obligation*, Book 1, Chapters 5-28. See also Thomas Aquinas, *Summa Theologica*, I-II, Questions 55-70. Josef Pieper's *Four Cardinal Virtues* is an excellent twentieth-century treatment of the virtues.

Wisdom/Cleverness
On the distinction between wisdom and cleverness, see Aristotle's discussion in his *Nicomachean Ethics*, Book 6, Chapter 13. The wise person is guided by the moral virtues (justice, courage, and moderation). Without these virtues, the person can be said to be shrewd or clever, but not wise. Cicero makes the same point in his work *On Moral Obligation*, Chapter 19. See also Augustine's discussion of the relation between wisdom and peace in *City of God*, Book

19, Chapter 20. Only if wisdom guides us (embracing prudence, courage, moderation, and justice), can we arrive at the fullness of peace.

Wonder/Bewilderment

On wonder as the root of all questioning and philosophy, see Aristotle, *Metaphysics,* Book 1, Chapter 2. It is human nature to wonder about the world around us and our place in it. See also G. K. Chesterton's Introduction to his *Everlasting Man.* Here he says that, in looking at the world and our place in it, we need to recover the elementary wonder of the child. Existence itself is a wonder, and it is particularly wonderful to be an intelligent being with the freedom to create. In *Orthodoxy,* Chapter 4: "The Ethics of Elfland," Chesterton points to the elementary wonder and gratitude of the child as the heart of all real virtue.

Biographical note

Montague Brown

Montague Brown came late to the joys of philosophy: after he completed his undergraduate degree in English Literature at the University of California at Berkeley in 1978, his wife gave him a copy of *The Collected Dialogues of Plato* for Christmas. Plato's quest for truth and all-encompassing intellectual honesty soon had Brown hooked on philosophy.

Brown moved on from Plato to devour the works of Aristotle, Augustine, and Aquinas. After avidly reading the entire text of Aquinas's more than 2,000-page *Summa Theologica,* he decided to undertake the formal study of philosophy and received a Ph.D. in philosophy from Boston College in 1986.

Literature and its real-life preoccupations — such as those in *The One-Minute Philosopher* — have always loomed large in Dr. Brown's philosophical work. He has served as chair of the Commission on the Arts at St. Anselm College in New Hampshire, where he teaches courses involving John Milton's *Paradise Lost* and Dante's *Commedia.* Dr. Brown has lectured on everything from *Antigone* and *Hamlet* to *Zen and the Art of Motorcycle Maintenance.*

In 1993 he published a characteristically practical book entitled *The Romance of Reason: An Adventure in the Thought of Thomas Aquinas.* In 1996 he followed up with a matter-of-fact ethics book, *The Quest for Moral Foundations.*

An amiable raconteur and an accomplished bassist — as well as a professor of philosophy at St. Anselm College for more than fifteen years — Dr. Brown lives in Weare, New Hampshire, with his wife, Meeta, and their four children.

Persons quoted

Joseph Addison (1672-1719), English essayist and poet.

Aeschylus (c. 525-456 B.C.), Greek writer of tragedies.

Aristotle (384-322 B.C.), Greek philosopher.

W. H. Auden (1907-1973), U.S. poet.

Augustine (354-430), Bishop of Hippo.

Francis Bacon (1561-1626), English philosopher, essayist, and statesman.

Boethius (c. 480-c. 524), Roman philosopher.

Jean de la Bruyère (1645-1696), French writer.

Miguel de Cervantes (1547-1616), Spanish novelist, poet, and playwright.

G. K. Chesterton (1874-1936), English essayist, novelist, and poet.

Winston Churchill (1874-1965), British statesman, writer, and Prime Minister.

Cicero (106-43 B.C.), Roman statesman, orator, and philosopher.

W. K. Clifford (1845-1879), British philosopher.

William Sloane Coffin, Jr., social activist.

Confucius (c. 551-c. 479 B.C.), Chinese philosopher and teacher.

Moncure D. Conway (1832-1907), U.S. writer and abolitionist.

James Fenimore Cooper (1789-1851), U.S. novelist.

Dante Alighieri (1265-1321), Italian poet.

Charles de Gaulle (1890-1970), French statesman and president.

William Drummond (1585-1649), Scottish poet.

John Dewey (1859-1952), U.S. philosopher and educator.

Diogenes Laertius (early third century), biographer of ancient Greek philosophers.

Fyodor Dostoyevsky (1821-1881), Russian novelist.

Frederick Douglass (1817-1895), U.S. black leader, journalist, and statesman.

Albert Einstein (1879-1955), U.S. physicist.

Dwight D. Eisenhower (1890-1969), U.S. president.

Epictetus (c. 50-c. 135), Greek Stoic philosopher.

Henry Fairlie (1924-1990), British writer.

George Farquhar (1678-1707), Irish playwright.

Richard P. Feynman (1918-1988), U.S. physicist.

Thomas Fuller (1654-1734), English writer and physician.

Solomon Ibn Gabirol (c. 1021-1058), Jewish poet and philosopher.

Germain Grisez (b. 1929), moral theologian.

G. W. F. Hegel (1770-1831), German philosopher.

Lewis B. Hershey (1893-1977), U.S. army general.

David Hume (1711-1776), Scottish philosopher.

Robert M. Hutchins (1899-1977), U.S. educator.

Thomas Jefferson (1743-1826), U.S. statesman and president.

John Paul II (b. 1920), Pope from 1978.

Samuel Johnson (1709-1784), English lexicographer, writer, and critic.

Immanuel Kant (1724-1804), German philosopher.

Thomas à Kempis (c. 1380-1471), ascetical writer.

Martin Luther King, Jr. (1929-1968), U.S. clergyman and civil rights leader.

Charles Kingsley (1819-1875), English writer and cofounder of the Christian Socialist movement.

C. S. Lewis (1898-1963), English writer.

Abraham Lincoln (1809-1865), U.S. president.

Toussaint L'Ouverture (c. 1743-1803), Haitian liberator and general.

Martin Luther (1483-1546), leader of the Protestant Reformation in Germany.

Russell Lynes (b. 1910), U.S. editor and critic.

Malcolm X (1925-1965), U.S. civil rights leader.

Jacques Maritain (1882-1973), French philosopher.

George C. Marshall, U.S. army general.

Miriam Makeba (b. 1932), South African singer.

J. S. Mill (1806-1873), English philosopher and economist.

John Milton (1608-1674), English poet.

Michel Eyquem de Montaigne (1533-1592), French essayist.

Alfred Armand Montapert (b. 1906), author.

John Henry Newman (1801-1890), English theologian, cardinal, and leader of the Oxford Movement.

Kane O'Hara (d. 1782), Irish playwright.

Blaise Pascal (1623-1662), French mathematician, physicist, and philosopher.

Plato (c. 427-c. 347 B.C.), Greek philosopher.

Arthur Wing Pinero (1855-1934), English playwright.

Alexander Pope (1688-1744), English poet.

Eleanor Roosevelt (1884-1962), U.S. writer, UN delegate, and first lady.

Theodore Roosevelt (1858-1919), U.S. president.

Roger Rosenblatt, contributing editor for *Time* and *New Republic* and public-television commentator.

Jean-Jacques Rousseau (1712-1778), French political philosopher and writer.

Josiah Royce (1855-1916), U.S. philosopher.

John Ruskin (1819-1900), English writer, art critic, and social reformer.

Bertrand Russell (1872-1970), philosopher, mathematician, and writer.

Bill Russell, Celtics basketball player and coach.

Seneca (c. 4 B.C.-A.D. 65). Roman philosopher, dramatist, and statesman.

William Shakespeare (1564-1616), English poet and dramatist.

Russell Shaw (b. 1935), journalist and author.

Frank Sheed (1897-1981), English Catholic apologist, writer, and founder of the publishing house Sheed and Ward.

Edith Sitwell (1887-1964), English poet and critic.

Socrates (c. 470-399 B.C.), Athenian philosopher and teacher.

Sophocles (c. 496-406 B.C.), Greek writer of tragic dramas.

Edmund Spenser (c. 1552-1599), English poet.

Adlai Stevenson (1900-1965), U.S. Democratic politician.

Jonathan Swift (1667-1745), English satirist.

Thomas Aquinas (c. 1225-1274), Dominican philosopher and theologian.

Henry David Thoreau (1817-1862), U.S. naturalist and writer.

Thucydides (c. 460-c. 400 B.C.), Athenian historian.

Alexis de Tocqueville (1805-1859), French author and statesman.

Abraham Tucker (1705-1774), English philosopher.

Luc de Clapiers Vauvenargues (1715-1747), French moralist and essayist.

Gore Vidal (b. 1925), U.S. novelist, playwright, and screenwriter.

Alice von Hildebrand (b. 1923), U.S. writer, teacher, and lecturer, born in Belgium.

Dietrich von Hildebrand (1889-1977), German philosopher, teacher, and writer.

Alice Walker (b. 1944), U.S. writer, civil-rights activist, and Pulitzer Prize winner.

George Washington (1732-1799), first U.S. president.

Elie Wiesel (b. 1928), U.S. writer, born in Romania.

Thornton Wilder (1897-1975), U.S. novelist and playwright.

Woodrow Wilson (1856-1924), U.S. president.

Oprah Winfrey, actress and talk-show host.

John Wooden, former UCLA basketball coach.

William Wordsworth (1770-1850), English poet laureate.

Index

Sophia Institute Press®

Sophia Institute™ is a nonprofit institution that seeks to restore man's knowledge of eternal truth, including man's knowledge of his own nature, his relation to other persons, and his relation to God. Sophia Institute Press® serves this end in numerous ways: it publishes translations of foreign works to make them accessible for the first time to English-speaking readers; it brings out-of-print books back into print; and it publishes important new books that fulfill the ideals of Sophia Institute™. These books afford readers a rich source of the enduring wisdom of mankind.

Sophia Institute Press® makes these high-quality books available to the general public by using advanced technology and by soliciting donations to subsidize its general publishing costs. Your generosity can help Sophia Institute Press® to provide the public with editions of works containing the enduring wisdom of the ages. Please send your tax-deductible contribution to the address below. We also welcome your questions, comments, and suggestions.

For your free catalog, call:
Toll-free: 1-800-888-9344

or write:
Sophia Institute Press®
Box 5284, Manchester, NH 03108

or visit our website:
www.sophiainstitute.com

Sophia Institute™ is a tax-exempt institution
as defined by the Internal Revenue Code,
Section 501(c)(3). Tax I.D. 22-2548708.